PAY YOURSELF
TO
WEALTH

Your guide to financial growth

By Steve Earl

ISBN 978-0-615-52870-0

Printed in the United States

Published by PSS Publishing
4227 Lafayette Center Drive
Chantilly, VA 20124

A message from the author:

I hope you enjoy the information in this book. I was passionate about writing this book, since the information has such a deep impact on all of our lives. There are many fine financial professionals that are interested in helping you achieve your goals and dreams. I encourage you to speak with a financial professional that can assist you in your planning.

Sincerely,

Steve Earl

Financial Guidance That Works

Hello, I am sure you will enjoy this easy to read book. Steve Earl tells a story about two families. One is a borrower and the other is a lender. You will learn the difference in these two strategies and the outcome for the families.

I have been teaching this strategy since about 1995 when I first learned how to set up this Unique Asset.

To get the best results you need an agent who understands how to design the plan for you.

Also you need to use a Mutual Insurance Company because the policy holders own the company.

I'm here to help any way I can, Cliff Crail

CONTENTS

Chapter 1

Once upon a time

Once upon a time, there were two young boys that grew up together attending the same school, playing in the same baseball league, and eventually even going to the same college. Johnny, the first boy, grew up just on the edge of the county line in a moderately-priced middle income neighborhood. His parents both worked good jobs, affording them the time to spend each weekend with Johnny and his older sister. Johnny's parents were very loving and stopped at nothing to provide him with all the resources possible. They volunteered their time to the school PTA. They always made sure Johnny did his homework, and they strived to teach their children the principles of hard work.

With such a nurturing family, Johnny easily kept himself on the right path. He always earned good grades, never caused problems, and even received a few trophies from his high school athletics. At the age of 18, along with all his classmates, Johnny excitedly sent out college applications to his choice of schools. Although not at the top of his class,

Johnny was confident that his grades would earn him acceptance to his desired colleges.

Sure enough, after a few weeks he started receiving acceptance letters. Now that he had been accepted, he needed to take care of the financial burden of attending a four-year program. He might even need to extend to six years, if his chosen career required more education. Luckily for Johnny, although his parents did not have much discretionary income, they could help him with the cost of some living expenses, and the remainder of his tuition and fees would be covered by his student loans. After five years of hard work, Johnny graduated college with a Master's degree in communications. Soon after graduating, Johnny landed a good entry-level job at a prestigious advertising firm making $40,000 annually. Johnny was on top of the world: young, energetic, and making a whopping $40,000 annually, straight out of school. Johnny knew he had more than enough to live and cover his now $430 monthly student loan bill, which would be paid in full over the next 15 years.

The second boy in our story, Adam, grew up in a very similar situation to Johnny's. In fact, they were good friends throughout school, and had decided to go to the same college – they even got hired to work at the same advertising agency. One could confuse them as brothers, as their demeanors were very similar. Adam's parents lived closer to the center of town, in an older, more exclusive neighborhood. His father was the President of the community bank, and had deep roots in the community, as his grandfather had started the community bank many years earlier. Although Adam's family came from money, and his father made a very good living as the community banker, they were not ones to flaunt their affluence. Hearing the news that his friend Johnny had been accepted into the same school, Adam thrilled at the prospect that they would be rooming together and taking many of the same courses.

Upon hearing the good news, Adam's father made him a deal. Rather than Adam taking out a student loan, he would let Adam borrow the money needed to pay for school, provided that upon graduation, Adam would promptly start paying $430 monthly into an account at the bank for the next fifteen years. After fifteen years, his dad would take back the initial $45,000 loan, and Adam could keep what was left. Adam was no dummy, and after some quick math, he calculated that he would have over $32,000 left in the account.

That's when his father told him,

"Son, always remember... never be the borrower; always be the lender. The rich lend the money; the poor always borrow it."

It was no surprise that fifteen years later both Johnny and Adam were still good friends; however, Johnny could never quite understand how Adam could always afford to live in a better home, and drive a better car. One day, many years later, Adam revealed to Johnny that he was going to take an early retirement to enjoy other passions. A baffled Johnny, knowing that they both had similar jobs and salaries, asked Adam how it was possible to have saved enough money.

"It's simple." Adam replied, with a smile on his face as he remembered the words of his father. "I never borrowed money. I always lent money to myself, and paid myself interest. It's amazing how much money you can either pay yourself or pay someone else. I just chose to pay myself."

And with that, Adam began to explain to Johnny how he had been able to make the decisions in life that put him on a prosperous financial path.

Chapter 2

Some basic truths

The story of Adam and Johnny is common in today's world. How we're taught to view finances establishes a pattern that follows us the rest of our lives. Johnny seemingly did everything right. He was a good student, graduated college, and held a good job; yet he was never able to keep up with Adam. Johnny followed societal norms. He did what his parents had done, what the financial institutions recommended, and what his financial advisers had told him. The truths that were never explained to Johnny were the same concepts that gave Adam such an advantage in life. An advantage that started with one basic principle:

"Never be the borrower; always be the lender."

Now that phrase seems simple enough, and if it were really that easy, why wouldn't everyone learn how to use it? The truth is buried deep in the fabric of our society. Everywhere you look, you are constantly asked to be a borrower. An easy experiment will illustrate this point. On any given day, count the number of store credit cards, gas cards, and other borrower offers that you receive. Every time you purchase an item, the clerk is directed to ask if you would be interested in a store credit card. Most will even go as far as baiting you with a discount on the purchase, if you complete the application. It all sounds very tempting and it's meant to be. Look in your wallet or purse. How many credit cards do you have? Is the number more than four?

Why do we borrow?

Like Johnny, most Americans have the desire to better their lives. The American promise of achieving our dreams, and living "the good life," is fueled by our hard work. It's the accumulation of our assets such as cars, homes, jewelry, and clothes that allows us to visualize our progress on the road to fulfilling the American dream. Unfortunately, too many of us have confused the measurement of success with the size and quantity of our possessions. After all, we can see an expensive car, a big home, or the motor boat, but we can't see what someone has in their savings account. Our friends and neighbors praise us for what they see, and we attach our success to that praise. With the ability to purchase assets on credit, it has become far too easy to falsely reward ourselves. Our ability to create debt has allowed us to surround ourselves with a false sense of success, and like Johnny, we inadvertently create a life of borrowing.

The average American household carries more than four credit cards. One in seven households has more than ten credit cards. The average American has $4300 in credit card debt. This is on top of student loans, car loans, mortgages, and other financed purchases. With so many offers constantly bombarding our lives, it's no wonder America has become a nation of borrowers. All this borrowing comes on the heels of one of the lowest savings rates in American history. The average American saves less than 1% of their income, while the average credit card interest rate in 2010 was just over 14%. Americans are literally going backwards from the day they turn 18 until the day they die. In other words, from the day they start working and earning an income until the day they stop earning an income, Americans are paying out more money than they take in.

The propaganda machine

How did this all happen? Why aren't we able to stop borrowing? The answer is all around us in the media, television, magazines and all the other day-to-day propaganda. The propaganda machine affects our lives in even deeper ways. Our friends, family, and neighbors are also intertwined in its mass broadcast. Unknowingly, those closest to us perpetuate the propaganda message, and are sometimes even rewarded by it. Your realtor convinced you to buy a bigger home; after all, the interest rates are so low on these new programs. Your mortgage broker convinced you to lower your payments by refinancing to a new mortgage. Your neighbor just told you about a great sale the department store was having, as she gloated about the new outfit she was wearing. It is all around us, and everywhere we look its effects can be seen.

But how did Adam manage to save more than Johnny? After all, didn't he have a nicer car, bigger home and earlier retirement than Johnny? How was it possible for Adam to achieve all this on the same income? Surely Adam must have been given a financial gift from his wealthy family. Isn't that how the rich really get rich...they inherit it? At least, that's what we're made to believe. The rich are rich because they had a head start. They are given money by their family. With such a financial advantage, it would seem that the only way for the average American to grow wealth is to borrow money. This would all seem logical, except for the fact that statistics dispute this way of thinking. According to a study of the Federal Reserve data, less than 10% of millionaires inherited their wealth. That means that over 90% of all wealthy Americans accumulated their money without gifts or inheritances. What is probably the most revealing statistic is that only 2% of American Households have a net worth of over $1 million, while over 25% of households have zero net worth.

Such skewed trends in the distribution of wealth in our country seem unnatural. After all, America was built on the principles of a strong middle class, not the archaic class system of the haves and have-nots. And statistics show that wealth is still self-made in America, so there must be a reason why some are able to accumulate wealth, while others are not. Could it be a secret formula for wealth accumulation? Have the top 2% of Americans figured out a recipe for wealth that is not being shared? And if so…what is it?

The answer to those questions is further revealed in yet another statistic. Outside of 401k and employer-sponsored plans, only 20% of Americans own individual stocks and less than 12% own bonds. To look at it another way, less than 20% of Americans are lenders, meaning they lend their money to corporations via stock purchases or bonds in return for a yield, while over 80% of Americans only borrow. This is the secret formula. The slight difference in the way we think about money shapes our choices, and puts us on either a path of prosperity or debt. The wealthy 2% have discovered that it is better to lend than to borrow. They have taught themselves the formula to using the propaganda machine to their advantage: eliminating debt, increasing earnings, and still enjoying all the fruits of society.

Physician or plumber?

The secrets of lender and borrower run deep in our cultural fabric. They do not discriminate by race, nationality, gender, or career choice. In fact, it's shocking to learn that in a comparison of actual take-home income, the average plumber in America will take home approximately the same amount of net income as a family physician over a thirty-year span. This seems highly unlikely given the fact that in 2009 the average family physician in America earned $141,000 annually versus $49,870 for the plumber, according to the U.S. Department of Labor. It's the need to fund education through borrowing that reduces the physician's ability to keep his income, thus putting him on par with the plumber.

Let's look at the lives of both professions from age 20 to 50. A plumber will earn an average of $49,870 annually over the course of his career. A family physician will earn an average $141,000 annually once in private practice, typically around the age of 33. This may seem like a good income, but by the time the average physician is out of medical school, has completed residency training, and starts a practice, he or she has spent over $300,000 on his or her education.

If during the years of training the physician had been working with the same income as a plumber, he would have made $648,000. Add the income lost by not working with the cost of education, and at age 33 the physician is a whopping $948,000 behind the plumber. If we then average the total income of each profession over a thirty-year period, subtracting the debt and taxes, the plumber's income is $34,000 compared to $36,000 for a physician.

The realities of wealth accumulation are often blurred by our preconceived notions. A plumber earns the same as a physician. A school teacher has the same opportunities to grow wealth as a lawyer, and everything we think we know about wealth is turned upside down. After all, if we already had the right understanding of true wealth accumulation, this book would not be necessary. For this reason, a change in personal wealth starts with an understanding of how our money works for us or against us. An understanding of this path to prosperity governed Adam's decisions about saving, investing, and creating wealth. And although he did not inherit any wealth from his family, Adam inherited the principles of lender and borrower.

The wealthy lend

It is clear that borrowing has become a social norm in today's world, but the wealthy segment of America thinks about borrowing very differently. In the simplest terms: the wealthy lend; the poor borrow. This is the most fundamental difference in how the wealthy think about money. The reasons that lead to the difference in our thinking start with the motivations of our financial institutions. It is in the interest of the banks, finance companies, and even merchants, to lend you money to buy their goods and services. The incentives to lend are so great that one of the largest propaganda machines in the history of mankind has been created. It's the propaganda that you can live a better life, be happier, feel better about yourself, if you buy that large home (but only if you take a 30 year mortgage), drive that new car (only if you lease it, of course), and of course, treat yourself to a five-star vacation (just put in on your credit card).

The propaganda machine is in full swing, and working every day. Turn on the television and see... It's not just in the advertisements, but watch how many television programs revolve around dressing well, wearing expensive jewelry, eating at expensive restaurants, and the list goes on. But wait. You don't watch those types of shows. You watch educational programming. In fact, just last week, you learned how to remodel a bathroom and the week before that, you learned about the Italian culture from a travel documentary on Rome. Wait...now that you think about it...you did mention to your best friend how great it would be to take a vacation to Italy. And the trip to the hardware store to buy a new faucet for your bathroom...well, maybe that was all just coincidental.

Your surroundings directly influence all of the choices about money you make. Since we don't live in a world by ourselves, our ability to distinguish good financial information from bad is clouded by the voices around us. It's for this reason that you must learn to recognize the negative influences, and fight to stay on a proper financial path.

Chapter 3

A compass for the road

The evidence clearly shows the differences in wealth among Americans can be partially attributed to the fact that the wealthy lend and the poor borrow. It's not a leap of faith to say that the goal of wealth can be obtained by thinking like a lender. But in order to change your financial path, you need to understand the decision-making concepts that can lead to better purchasing and savings decisions. Our ability to think like a lender begins by understanding:

1. how to recognize wrong steps;
2. the difference between cost and price, and;
3. the value of time.

You are not excluded

Changing the way we manage money and learning to think like the wealthy sounds reasonable and simple, but is it?

Can anyone change their position in life from becoming a borrower to becoming a lender? It all sounds like fantasy, a pipe dream, like many other get-rich quick schemes that end up leaving followers worse than when they started. And even if there were a legitimate way to choose a better path, one free from debt that allowed us to grow wealth, that choice is long gone for those of us that already have a mortgage, credit card debts, and other financial obligations. If it were possible to restart a person's financial future, maybe it would only apply to lawyers, doctors, accountants, business owners, and not plumbers, electricians, or everyday workers. Maybe it's a great philosophy, even the most central reason why the rich are rich and the poor stay poor, but like many choices we make in life, it cannot be reversed, and is a choice that should have been made earlier in life.

It can sound daunting, even impossible, the idea of changing our behavior in order to re-chart our course to wealth. But, the truth is somewhere in between. It's always going to be easier to start on the correct path to wealth when the choice is made in your youth, before mortgages, credit cards, and student loans. And of course, the younger the person, the more time he has to accumulate wealth. However, we can choose at any time to become a lender or a borrower. Obtaining financial freedom and staying on the correct path to wealth has little to do with your career choice or educational background. Even our current debt level has very little bearing on our choice.

The reasons we conjure up in our minds as to why it's not possible to change, to adopt a new and correct philosophy on wealth accumulation, result from the vices taught to us through the propaganda machine. That's right. From childhood, Americans have been implanted with the false propaganda that we must borrow in order to live a better life. We must fight against our own negativity that we cannot empower ourselves to learn the correct path to financial well-being. And with this new empowerment, we will realize that this change in ideology is not some get-rich quick scheme, offering wealth without effort, but instead, a life transformation that will take us off the wrong path and put us on the path to wealth. From this point forward we are going to choose to think like a lender, not a borrower.

Wrong steps

As with any journey, when we follow the wrong path, we should retrace and recognize the errors in our last steps, and then follow the new guide of our compass. One of the most misunderstood and misleading steps we make involves not what we purchase, but the way in which we make the purchase. Most people make this mistake, including many financial counselors that seek to help their clients get back on track. It's not the decision we make to buy the new automobile, upgrade our house, or even purchase the television at the local department store that gets us in trouble financially. Many consumers are fiscally savvy enough to know that before making a big purchase, they should always compare prices. After all, you wouldn't go buy a new car without negotiating the price, or even comparing the prices at a few different dealerships.

Most shoppers are frugal and want the best deal. If this were not the case, stores wouldn't spend the time to lure shoppers in with promotional discounts and coupons. People understand the need to save money, and most shoppers do a diligent job at price analysis. But people seeking financial rehabilitation mistakenly focus on the wrong part of their spending behavior. This misunderstanding is why so many people fail to ever improve their situation. They continue to try to resolve the wrong problems, ultimately conceding to failure and going back on a destructive path.

COST not PRICE

Focusing on *price*, not *cost*, is the error made by so many Americans seeking to climb their way out of debt. This sad reality can be witnessed over and over, as more Americans face foreclosure and even bankruptcy. As hard as borrowers may try, overcoming spending habits is next to impossible if they don't understand the difference between cost and price. This is a fundamental difference in thinking between a lender and a borrower. A borrower always looks at price. What is the price of this television? What will my monthly payments be? What is the price of the extended warranty?

So exactly what are the differences? The price of an item is what you pay for that item if you are able to pay in cash, and without any other future obligations attached to that item. Later in this book, you will see that every item you purchase has a cost greater than its price. The cost of an item is the total amount of money, present and future, that you will spend in order to obtain that item. In fact, you can tell that most people have little idea of the difference between price and cost, as the two words are often used interchangeably. For example, if you purchase an automobile for $17,000, but then finance it over three years, the cost of the automobile would be $17,000 plus any finance charges.

This all goes back to the propaganda machine. Merchants do not want to illustrate the true cost of an item, when the price can appear so much lower. Remember, we are all inherently good at comparing the price of items.

Merchants and lenders know this. For this reason, a car dealer may advertise a low purchase price, and then try to sell you on a high interest rate loan. The dealer views his total profit based on his ability to get as much money from the sale as possible. This means that selling you a low-priced car is acceptable, if he can make more money from selling a higher-priced loan.

The cost of everything you buy is hidden by the price of the item. More often than not, the profit for the merchant and certainly the lender is in the cost of the item, not its price. This is why every major merchant offers store credit cards and instant financing. This is also why your local mortgage broker is taught to sell you the mortgage with the lowest monthly payment (another word for price). You will never see a successful merchant advertise the true cost of an item. This would be counterproductive, as you would be compelled to then compare the cost of his item to others.

Let me illustrate this point in a not so obvious setting. This is a setting that you would never think involved the propaganda machine. Have you ever wondered why the Lottery jackpot never advertises the actual payment stream? Instead, they advertise the "sum-of-all-payments?" What this means is that the $10 million jackpot does not actually pay out $10 million, but rather a choice of either monthly payments equal to $10 million over the course of many years, or a reduced lump sum of maybe $7 million.

Think of it this way (and trust me, the lottery ticket sellers have) – if you could choose between two lottery tickets, would you spend money on a $7 million jackpot, if you could buy a $10 million jackpot for the same ticket price? Probably not. You would buy the $10 million jackpot, because it would be a better price. The Lottery ticket sellers know this, so they advertise the larger jackpot amount, because it makes the price seem better. In essence, you are getting less than what is advertised. If you wanted a true $10 million jackpot, you would need to buy a more expensive ticket.

The lottery example is only used to illustrate the distinct differences between cost and price, and a small example of how it can be used to sway behavior. No one would analyze the cost of a lottery ticket, but what about the cost of that new television, the automobile, your mortgage, and even a student loan? The same principles apply, and the proper analysis of the cost of an item, not its price, can determine its true value to you. This is at the root of the mistake made by many financial counselors. They try to change a person's spending behavior, by insisting that they should not purchase the new automobile or the flat screen television. This approach obviously does not work, or everyone would be rehabilitated and content with their old items.

A far more effective approach is to teach yourself how to think like a lender, not a borrower, therefore allowing you to evaluate the cost of an item, not its price. Once you know the cost of an item, you will find yourself changing your spending habits as you properly re-evaluate your need for that item. Think of your last big purchase. Would you have purchased the same exact item if it had cost 30% more? 70% more? How about 100% more? Probably not. Odds are, you would have re-evaluated your choice, and selected a similar item with a lower price.

Now you're starting to think like a lender!

Now you know

It's easier than ever to see the profound effect that your choice to think like a lender or borrower has had on your life. The evidence that the rich lend and that the poor borrow is all around us. The propaganda machine, through the use of media and social persuasion, continually pushes us to benefit lenders, not borrowers. Since we can now see that there are subtle yet very important differences in how lenders and borrowers think, and that the choice to change our financial outlook can be made by anyone at any time, we can begin to learn the tools to put us on the right path. The importance of understanding the next few concepts will transform your ability to make purchasing and saving decisions. These ideas are not new and certainly not a secret among financial professionals, but the way in which we use them and apply them is drastically different if you are thinking like a borrower versus a lender.

Chapter 4

Double your money

It's easy to see how we can all do better saving money, and controlling our spending habits. We can even put into practice tools to help us recognize where we have gone wrong in the past, so that we don't repeat mistakes. But although these ideas help us understand what we should do with our money, they don't tell us the impact our decisions have on our money. This is why we must empower ourselves with a tool that can help us calculate the effects that spending, borrowing, and saving have on us. This is where the Money Doubling Rule, better known within financial circles as the Rule of 72, comes into play. The Rule of 72 allows you to quickly calculate the time it will take to double your money based on the interest rate you earn.

For example, if you saved $1000 at a 6% annual interest rate, you'd double your money in 12 years. 72 divided by 6 (6%) is 12 (12 years). That means in 12 years your $1000 investment will be worth $2000. This is one of the most powerful quick financial calculations you can remember.

The Rule of 72 can help you understand the true cost of an item, by allowing you to calculate how much money you will pay out on a financed purchase based on an offered interest rate. Let's assume that your revolving credit card balances are $4500 with an average interest rate of 14%. If you divide 72 by 14, you get 5 years. That means that every five years you are paying the lender 100% of the initial purchase price, just in interest. It's a great deal if you are the lender. Another way to look at it is that every five years, the television you purchased using your store credit card at a price of $500, is actually costing you $1000.

Now, what if you paid off your credit card at the end of the month? Then certainly, that television was no more expensive than $500. And aren't we forgetting about the payments we make every month; shouldn't that be taken into consideration? All of those factors would certainly matter, but the reality is that although we make payments each month, most borrowers continue to purchase new items, thereby replenishing the debt. Think of your credit cards. You probably have store cards that somehow seem to always have the same balance from month to month, even though you diligently make your payments. This is an old lender secret. The lender knows that most borrowers will continue to replenish the debt, meaning they continue to borrow at the same rate that they pay back debt. This is why the average American household maintains a steady debt balance, even as they earn more and increase their debt payments.

The effects of interest, as illustrated by the Rule of 72, really work in the lender's favor. The lender knows that the earnings they make from the steady balances are not affected by the flow of payments in and out of the accounts. If, for example, you are maintaining a steady balance of, let's say $5,000...then the rule of 72 will always apply. At

7%, the Lender will double its money every 10 years and at 14%, it will double every 5 years. No matter what you do...increase your payments...lower your interest rate... as long as you are maintaining a steady balance, the lender will continue to periodically double their money. Never forget, the lender will always come out ahead.

Knowing the Rule of 72, and understanding how to utilize it every time you're selecting a payment method on your purchases, will prevent you from under-estimating the true cost. If you are using anything other than cash (debit card) for your purchase, then you must calculate the true cost.

Wealth Exercise #1

Here is an effective exercise to better understand your purchases. Once you complete a Rule of 72 chart on your credit cards, you will see that each of your purchases using a credit card contributes to your debt cycle, and the true cost of the purchase is much greater than the initial price paid. Complete the following chart for your credit cards/ store cards:

Rule of 72 Chart

	Interest Rate	Balance	Rule of 72 Calculation	True COST on purchases
My Visa	14%	$3000	72 Divided by (14) = 5 Years	COST doubles every 5 Years
Electronic Store Card	12.9%	$1300	72 Divided by (12.9) = 5.5 Years	COST doubles every 5.5 years
Other Card	13.5%	$1200	72 Divided by (13.5) = 5.3 Years	COST doubles every 5.3 years

Now you're armed

Understanding the rule of 72, and how it applies to you as a borrower, is quite liberating, but knowing how to use it as a lender is awe-inspiring. Remember, as a lender the Rule of 72 tells you how long it will take to double your money at a given interest rate. Armed with that simple information, you can begin to value many investments. And since we are now thinking like a lender, every time we put money in a savings account, a money market, a retirement plan, or any other savings vehicle, we can quickly assess how long it will take to grow our money.

A key point to understand is that investing our money, whether in a savings account or mutual fund, is in essence lending. We deposit (we can also say lend or invest) our money and in return, depending on the type of account/investment product, the recipient pays us to use our money. That payment, more often than not, is in the form of an interest rate or dividend payment. If we deposit $1000 in an investment that pays 6% interest, then the rule of 72 says that we will double our money in 12 years. Exercising our knowledge of the Rule of 72 is a must before any purchase and/or any investment. Although it does not take into account the risk of an investment, it can quickly help us understand the benefit or cost of our decisions.

Chapter 5

Opportunity cost

Every asset you own and every dollar you make has two very distinct values attached to it:

1. the market value of the asset, and;
2. the value of its opportunity cost.

The opportunity cost is the amount of money we could earn if we invested the value of our item. Simply put, when we own an item, we are giving up the opportunity to take the value of that item and invest it. Let's say you own a television worth $1,000. If you could sell that television, and put the money in the bank earning 5%, you would earn $50 a year. The $50 you could be earning each year is the opportunity cost of the television.

Let's use, for example, $1000. The market value of $1000 is of course $1000, but the value of its opportunity cost may be much greater than $1000. If that $1000 could be invested at 6% annually, the opportunity cost would be

$60 annually. Over a ten-year period the opportunity cost becomes $600 ($60 x 10).

The market value is what an item is worth if you were to sell it. Unfortunately, most items we purchase do not do a very good job at holding their market value. When is the last time you purchased a new car and a year later, could sell it for what you paid? If we're going to build wealth, then we must always think like a lender. Every dollar we spend and every purchase we make is an investment. And as lenders, we must always make a return on our investments. When we purchase items for pleasure (a common habit of the borrower,) we are using our money at a 0% return. And again, let's not forget that more often than not, the items we purchase usually lose value to the point where they are worth nothing.

Every item we purchase or currently own has a market value and thus an opportunity cost. Even your house has an opportunity cost. This is the primary reason why a home should never be considered an investment. The opportunity cost far exceeds our ability to gain a good return. What's worse is that not only are we losing the opportunity cost of each dollar that is sitting in our home, but also lose the opportunity cost of the money we pay in interest to our mortgage holder.

Minimize the opportunity cost

Our goal as a lender should always be to minimize the opportunity cost of our assets. In other words, we want to squeeze out as much return as possible from every asset, balanced with our tolerance for risk. An asset with zero opportunity cost is an asset that is returning the maximum amount possible. Imagine if in the example above, our $1000 was sitting under our mattress, instead of in a bank. The opportunity cost of that $1000 is at its highest level. We are earning nothing on it. On the other hand, if we could get 6% interest annually in a slightly higher risk investment, but we chose to keep it in a savings account paying 2%, then our opportunity cost has certainly decreased from the money sitting under the mattress. The opportunity cost at 2%, however, is still higher than if we had invested it at 6%.

It now seems obvious that both examples of cash and home carry the burden of opportunity cost. But if we are to think like lenders, then we must accept that every item we possess or wish to possess has an opportunity cost attached to it. This leads to the common misperception that if you have an asset completely paid for, then it doesn't cost anything. How often have you heard this? I have two cars, but my second car is paid for so it does not cost anything. Or, I have a boat, but it's paid for so it doesn't cost me anything. Or, we just paid off our vacation home, so it does not cost us anymore. Those are the words of a borrower, as they relate the cost of their assets to the repayment of debt. A lender looks at every asset owned and asks the following question: If the value of this asset were invested, how much money would I be making? Understanding the opportunity cost of ownership can help us determine whether we are living beyond our means, or simply not properly accounting for the true cost of an item.

Let's look at an example to clarify this point. Let's suppose Johnny, our borrower from chapter one, makes $40,000 annually. He lives in an apartment paying $1000 monthly in rent and drives a used car. He is able to live comfortably, but does not have much money left over for savings. One day Johnny's uncle passes away, leaving him a cabin on a lake worth $350,000. Since the lake home is fully paid and the maintenance costs are minimal, Johnny decides to keep the property as an investment.

What Johnny has not taken into consideration in his decision to keep the lake home is the opportunity cost of his new asset. Johnny's decision to keep the lake-front home is costing him money each year, money that he would earn if he invested the proceeds from the sale. If Johnny could earn 6% interest by investing the sales price of the home, he would make over $21,000 a year. Considering that he only earns $40,000 annually from his job, it suddenly seems unwise for him to be losing $21,000 a year on a lake home.

Whether confronted with decisions to keep assets or simply evaluating our next purchase, understanding the opportunity cost of an item is essential. Never ignore the value of unused assets, such as second homes, cars, motorcycles, and boats. Always remember that the cost of ownership extends far beyond the debt pay-off date. Everything we own cost us money. As long as an asset has a market value, it has an opportunity cost. And as long as it has an opportunity cost, then it is costing you real money.

An interesting exercise can be made by adding up all of your assets, and determining their opportunity cost. It is surprising how much money it cost us to own all of our possessions. The next time you purchase a big item, consider the opportunity cost in addition to the market cost of the item, before you make your purchase.

A simple rule to remember the next time you make a purchase: at 6% interest, for every $1000 spent, you are obligating yourself to spending an additional $60 a year for the rest of your life.

Now you're thinking like a Lender!

Chapter 6

Value of time

The rules that govern financial decisions are the same for both lenders and borrowers. After all, interest rate, loan amount, depreciation, value, debt, asset, and many of the other words used throughout our financial lives are the same for everyone. It's our interpretation of their meanings and more importantly, how we view their impact on us, which tells us whether we are thinking like a lender or a borrower. As we've seen in the previous chapters, it always comes down to choosing whether we want to look at financial decisions using the viewpoint of a lender or a borrower. One of the biggest differences in these viewpoints is the way we look at the concept of time.

Time is the most basic yet powerful element of money. It is the one variable that we cannot replenish in our financial lives. We can always search out for a better interest rate, a lower cost, and even a more suitable investment period, but we cannot reclaim lost time. This is fundamental to any debt financing, investment planning, or retirement plan. Thinking like a lender, our goal is always to maximize the return over the longest amount of time. The more you can lock-in a high return over a long period of time, the more profitable your investment; thus minimizing the opportunity cost of your investment. Remember, our goal as a lender is to maximize our return; thereby minimizing our assets' opportunity cost. This goal is vastly different than the goals of most borrowers. This is most evident when you look at the average mortgage length in America being 30 years. It isn't that borrowers don't have a choice of mortgage programs; in fact, there are many alternative mortgage loan programs such as a 15 year, but borrowers have never been taught to value time. Instead they purchase the program most recommended to them by – you guessed it – their lender. Isn't that a coincidence? The program that favors lenders the most happens to be the program that is purchased most often by borrowers.

The disguise of lower payments

Borrowers incorrectly migrate towards low payment instead of shorter time periods. It is this borrowing premise that begins to define borrowing habits early in life. Although we are told to save a portion of our money, there is a contradictory notion that everyone should live within a budget. And although the basic premise of having a budget is correct, the meaning of budget is misunderstood. Budget is misinterpreted to mean that as long as we don't spend more than we earn, then we are succeeding at living within a budget. This error in thinking is further magnified by a borrower's manipulation of time, as they trade future earnings to reduce current expenditures; or in other words, lowering their monthly payments and extending the payment time frame.

Trading time is the worst financial decision that can be made. When you trade time for reduced payments, you trick yourself into a false sense of proper budgeting. This behavior is the glue lenders use to keep borrowers locked in. Remember, time is finite. You can't create more time. Everyone's ability to earn and invest is limited by time. If you begin to work at the age of 25 and wish to retire at the age of 65, then you are limited to a 40 year time frame. Once you begin trading those future years, approximately 40, in order to reduce current expenses, then you drastically limit your ability to ever stop borrowing.

This disastrous trade is made every day by unsuspecting Americans. The average age of a first-time home buyer in America is 30, with an average mortgage of $167,000, resulting in $1200 monthly payments for 30 years. For purposes of discussion, let's go back to Johnny, and let's assume he had a $167,000 mortgage with $1200 monthly payments. If Johnny never upgraded residences, and diligently made every monthly mortgage payment, he would pay off the balance of his mortgage at age 60. That would leave Johnny only 5 years before he retired. If at age 60 Johnny began saving his $1200 monthly mortgage payment at 5% interest, he would have approximately $81,600 saved for retirement.

If we calculate how much Johnny spent on his mortgage over the last 30 years, we can see it was $432,000 ($1200 multiplied by 360 payments). It is easy to see that the lender came out ahead, with a gain of $265,000 ($432,000 sum of mortgage minus $167,000 borrowed).

Now let's suppose Adam, Johnny's friend, purchased a similar home. Adam understands the opportunity cost of his monthly payments. He understands that every mortgage payment he makes, he loses the opportunity to invest that money. But he also realizes that he needs a home, so contrary to the recommendations of his banker, Adam takes out a 15 year mortgage on the $167,000 he reluctantly borrows. The banker tells Adam that his payments would be $1580 monthly on a 15 year note.

Thinking like a lender, Adam accepts the 15 year mortgage, and diligently makes payments until he is 45 years of age. At age 45, Adam's mortgage will be paid off, allowing him to start saving for retirement. If he then saves the original $1200 monthly amount, assuming a 5% interest rate, he will have just over $493,000 saved by the time he is 65. If we calculate how much he spent on his mortgage over a 15 year period, we can see it was just over $284,000 ($1580 multiplied by 180 payments).

The comparison of both the 15 year and the 30 year mortgage options shows a remarkable difference. By reducing the trade of time by slightly increasing his monthly payment, Adam spends significantly less money on his mortgage than Johnny. Adam is also able to create a retirement fund in excess of $493,000. A side-by-side comparison makes it easy to seek how time can work against borrowers, and favors lenders on a typical mortgage.

15 Year or 30 Year Mortgage?

	Adam's 15 Year Loan	Johnny's 30 Year Loan
Loan Amount	$167,000	$167,000
Monthly Payment	$1580	$1200
Total COST of loan	$284,000	**$432,000**
Paid off at age	45	60
Years remaining to save for retirement	**20**	5
Amount saved at age 65 ($1200 monthly savings)	**$493,000**	$81,600

* Based on a 7.8% mortgage interest rate

The old adage "Time is Money" could not be more true.

Your time is a valuable asset; don't ever trade it for lower payments. Instead always work to maximize the amount of time your money is working for you.

Now you're thinking like a Lender!

Chapter 7

Four tools of wealth accumulation

It's clear that the way the wealthy think about money is vastly different than the way the poor think about money. Now that we have a new perspective on how the wealthy think, and we are armed with the tools that help us avoid the pitfalls of borrowing, we can begin to learn the tools used by lenders. It is these lending tools that enable the wealthy to keep accumulating wealth, by using the system to their advantage. These tools include

1. use of time;
2. importance of now;
3. staged savings, and;
4. the compounding of money.

As we've seen, this can be accomplished through interest rates, extension of time, and ultimately the ability to remain on the side of a lender by not exposing money to borrowing practices. It's the use of these lending tools that can transform anyone into a lender from a borrower. And as you will see, it is the income-producing elements of lending that really begin to amplify a lender's wealth.

Tool #1: Rethinking time

It's not only our choice to trade time for lower payments that can destroy our financial futures. We can also change our way of thinking about planning for future events. Humans mark the milestones in their lives' in a chronological timeline. Your first words, first baby steps, first day of school, getting a driver's license, high school graduation, starting a job, marriage, purchasing a home, starting a family, retirement. All of these life events coincide with our age, and thus we assign them a timeline in our minds. And although financial events may coincide with our chronological timeline, we can't make the mistake of prioritizing financial events based on where they fall in our timeline.

For example, if you ask a 25-year old which is more important for their age, to start saving for retirement or a new home, the resounding answer would be a new home. If you ask the same question to a 35-year old with a newborn child, she may reply, "neither," and insert the need to save for the child's college education. Yet if you ask a 55-year old, more often than not, he will answer with, "retirement."

The correct answer is…all of the above. As soon as an event becomes certain in your life, then that event begins to carry with it time (better understood as the time frame until the event happens.) Since we now understand that time has value, then we must make use of as much of that time as possible. This is an extremely important concept and one that cannot be stressed enough. Using retirement as an example, no one would argue that the earlier one starts saving, the better off one would be. It also makes sense that if parents want to save for their child's education, they are much better off to start when the child is born rather than waiting until high-school. This all seems like common sense...but it might surprise you to learn how valuable time really is.

Now let's fast-forward in Johnny's and Adam's lives, to the point where they become parents and decide to save for their children's education. If they each committed to saving $200 a month for 9 years to pay for their child's education, which parent would save more? That seems like a silly question. They would save the same amount, wouldn't they? What if Adam started saving $200 monthly for 9 years at his son's birth, and Johnny started saving once his child was nine years old? How much would they each have when their children are eighteen?

Assuming a steady 5% return, Adam's son will have over $42,000 saved for college, while Johnny's son will only have $27,000 saved. They each saved $200 monthly for 9 years (totaling $21,600), but Adam used all the time available to him, eighteen years to be exact. Johnny, however, wasted the first nine years before he began to save. Remember the Rule of 72: Adam was able to stop saving after the first 9 years, and was able to almost double what he had saved over the remaining nine years.

This example illustrates the power of time, and the need to always use as much time as we have before a financial event such as college, retirement, or homeownership occurs. This is why it's important to stop organizing financial events in a chronological order, and organize them in a current To-Do list as soon as an event becomes certain. This will require you to learn how to identify events that have become certain in your life. If you ever plan on retiring, then retirement is a certain event. If you want to purchase a home, then home ownership is a certain event. If you have a child and want to send them to college, then college savings is a certain event. Creating a financial to-do list and planning your savings goals will allow you to extract all the value of time, and help keep you thinking like a lender.

Wealth Exercise #2

As an exercise, try creating a to-do list based on your certain events. Calculate how much you must save in order to accomplish your goal. Now, to understand the effects that time has on your list, make a second list with the same exact events, except this time reduce the amount of time you have to save by half. Watch how much more difficult it will be to achieve your goal. You will notice how reducing the time in half for longer-term items such as a retirement has an exponential effect on the savings needed to meet the goal. It is this effect that makes lenders rich and keeps borrowers poor.

To-Do #1 *(assuming 5% interest rate)*

	Years to Event (TIME)	Goal	Monthly Savings Required
Down Payment for First Home	5	$25,000	$367
Becky's College Fund	17	$75,000	$233
Retirement	34	$500,000	$467

To-Do #2 *(assuming 5% interest rate)*

	Years to Event (TIME)	Goal	Monthly Savings Required
Down Payment for First Home	2.5	$25,000	$784
Becky's College Fund	8	$75,000	$636
Retirement	17	$500,000	$1559

Tool #2: The importance of NOW

In order to succeed, one must have a plan. Whether it's a sports team, business, or personal goal, success can never be achieved without proper planning. This is the beginning point for every lender. The goal of making as much money as possible with as little expense as possible starts with the development of a plan. And although everyone's financial circumstances are unique, the two primary elements of a good financial plan are often the same: the amount we can invest, and the amount we need to achieve a goal. Everything else regarding a financial plan will revolve in one way or another around one of those two elements.

If you think of the two elements of your financial plan in terms of time, the amount that you can invest is represented in the NOW of your plan. In other words, the amount you can invest right now. The total amount you need in order to achieve your goal (buying a house, college savings, retirement) is represented at the end point of your plan. Because we know that time is valuable, and that we can't afford to waste any of it, the NOW of our plan always represents what we can do at this moment. The amount we save now is flexible and can always be adjusted up or down as our finances permit. Just remember, thinking like a lender means we will never think about saving tomorrow or next month. We will never delay saving, and we will never sidestep our need to save in order to purchase something. Instead, we will always calculate the amount of money we can save now, and make adjustments to what we spend in order to save.

Knowing the two elements of your financial plan allows you to create a road map for achieving a financial goal. Once you determine the amount of money you can save now, you can easily determine how much you will have at the end of your plan. If the amount falls below your goal, then you simply adjust either your goal or the amount you save.

Tool #3: Staging your savings

In some situations you may find it difficult to achieve your goal based on your current ability to save. In these situations it is necessary to utilize a tool called *staging your savings*. Staging refers to enhancing your periodic (monthly, quarterly, annually) savings rate with an automatic increase in the amount you save.

For example, let's say that you are trying to save $18,000 for an automobile, and have calculated your need to save $300 monthly for five years, but only have the ability to initially save $200 monthly. If you adjust your plan to save $200 monthly for the first year, $250 monthly in year 2, $300 monthly in year 3, $350 monthly in year 4, and $400 monthly in year 5, you will still reach your $18,000 goal. Staging is a powerful tool that accommodates all financial situations, while eliminating any excuse to procrastinate the start of your plan.

Staging is also a fantastic way to realize large financial goals when you have the ability to utilize long periods of time. This is best seen in both college savings plans and retirement plans, where long periods of time can be used. A staging plan can dramatically increase the accumulation of savings versus an un-staged plan.

For example, if we compare the savings of two people using staged and un-staged methods of retirement savings, we can see dramatic differences in the end-point of their savings plan. If at age 35 Johnny decided to start saving $500 monthly towards retirement for the next 30 years, assuming a 5% interest rate, he would have $416,000. If Adam, on the other hand, were able to save the same $500 monthly, but could increase his monthly savings amount each year by $50, he would have over $854,000 at age 65. Staging allows you to meet large financial goals, while beginning the savings plan within any budget.

Tool #4: Compounding your money

Every lender knows that the real amplifier of their money is the effects of compounding. Compounding is what happens when you let your money make you more money.

For example, if you invested $1000 for one year compounded annually at 5% interest, you would have $1050 at the end of the year. Now if you were to take back your $1000, you could still invest the $50 you earned. It is the $50 left over ($1050 minus $1000 you invested) that really begins to make you money. At the same 5% interest, that $50 will earn you an additional $2.50 a year. What's even more powerful is that additional $2.50 you earned will begin to earn you another $0.13 a year and so on.

Compounding is such an extremely powerful lending tool that, used along side of time, it can make virtually any savings goal possible. The effects of compounding can easily illustrate how two similar income earners can have very different financial paths. If we were to compare the financial lives of both Johnny and Adam, we can better understand the effects compounding can have on them. Let's assume at age 35, both Johnny and Adam each made $65,000 annually, but Adam began to save $5000 each year for twenty years, while Johnny saved nothing.

The following table quickly illustrates how much extra income Adam had during the course of his life, even after he stopped saving. The key to understand is that the interest earnings illustrated in the chart represents income that Adam would have for the rest of his life. Even when Adam stops saving, he would continue to earn the interest income in addition to all of the money he had saved.

A Total Income Comparison: Adam Saving $5,000 per Year at 5% Interest

Year	Johnny's Salary	Adam's Salary Plus Interest Income From savings	Annual Interest at 5%
1	$65,000	$65,250	$250
2	$65,000	$65,520	$520
3	$65,000	$65,812	$812
4	$65,000	$66,127	$1,127
5	$65,000	$66,467	$1,467
6	$65,000	$66,834	$1,834
7	$65,000	$67,230	$2,230
8	$65,000	$67,659	$2,659
9	$65,000	$68,122	$3,122
10	$65,000	$68,621	$3,621
11	$65,000	$68,911	$3,911
12	$65,000	$69,224	$4,224
13	$65,000	$69,562	$4,562
14	$65,000	$69,926	$4,926
15	$65,000	$70,321	$5,321
16	$65,000	$70,746	$5,746
17	$65,000	$71,206	$6,206
18	$65,000	$71,703	$6,703
19	$65,000	$72,239	$7,239
20	$65,000	$72,818	$7,818

Chapter 8

Constructing your plan

The ability to construct a financial plan tailored to our individual situations is crucial to our long-term success. Recognizing the difference in perspective between a lender and a borrower, and understanding how to use the basic financial tools to empower us to save, are only the beginning of our journey. It is the creation, adoption, and maintenance of our financial plan that will ultimately enable us to not just think like a lender, but also to build wealth like a lender. And although everyone's financial road map will look different, the building blocks will be the same.

Our financial road map must comprise of three parts:

1. Reducing personal expenses;
2. Systematically directing income to savings, and;
3. Maintaining consistency in our financial behavior.

Road Map – Part 1: Reduce expenses

Reducing personal expenses can be the most challenging part of a financial plan, due to the need to modify our behaviors. We must modify our predisposition of thinking like a borrower and begin to always look at purchases as a lender. Unplanned purchases and purchases that have little long term value must always be re-evaluated with our newly acquired lender's perspective. If the item cannot be paid for in cash, then it must not be purchased. If the opportunity cost of the purchase is too great and we do not have an immediate need for the item, then we must fight the urge to spend, even if we have the cash. Reducing personal expenses also encompasses our need to pay for things we have purchased in the past, by reducing our existing debt. Reducing our debt will help increase our immediate income by reducing our interest expenses.

Road Map – Part 2: Systematically save

Little needs to be said about the importance of saving. From childhood we have been told to save for a rainy day, but we have never been taught how to save. It is the *how to save* that makes all the difference. How to save consists of the ability to determine the amount, duration and investment vehicle in which we choose to save. This sounds far more complicated than it needs to be. Everyone can save an amount. Whether it is $1 or $10,000, the amount you save should be determined by your ability to consistently save that same amount.

Consistency is the key to savings. Saving money consistently allows you to work your savings within a budget. It will also help you avoid the killer of all savings plans, procrastination. Consistently setting aside an amount for yourself each pay period will not only give you an easy starting point, but it will create a great savings base you can build from.

Let's say you were unsure how much money you could begin saving. If you still had credit card debt and other expenses that needed attention, you could start a low savings rate of $100 monthly. After a few months of budgeting, you might be in a better situation to evaluate an increase in your savings rate. With the use of staging as a savings tool, you could increase your savings rate every 6 months. Incrementally increasing your savings rate would allow you to adjust to a more desirable savings rate, without compromising your ability to meet current expenses. The most important part of selecting an amount is to select an amount and start your savings plan now. Too many people delay the start of a savings plan because they don't think they can save enough. The amount is never as important as the actual act of starting to save consistently. Remember, it's not where you start that determines where you end up.

Wealth Exercise #3

The following charts illustrate two basic savings plans with very different starting points. Without taking into account interest earnings, it is easy to see how two very different savings plans can yield almost the same results. Whether someone begins to save at a rate of $100 monthly or $450 monthly, the total amount saved at the end of the period has little to do with the beginning. With the use of tools such as staging, anyone can start saving at any time. You can quickly see how the end points are not determined by the start. Complete the empty chart for yourself, and see how much money you can begin saving. Try to stage your savings and see how much more wealth you can create over time.

Starting Point Savings Compared

Year	Monthly Savings Rate	Total Saved for Year	Monthly Savings Rate	Total Saved for Year
1	$100	$1,200	$450	$5,400
2	$125	$1,500	$450	$5,400
3	$150	$1,800	$450	$5,400
4	$175	$2,100	$450	$5,400
5	$200	$2,400	$450	$5,400
6	$225	$2,700	$450	$5,400
7	$250	$3,000	$450	$5,400
8	$275	$3,300	$450	$5,400
9	$300	$3,600	$450	$5,400
10	$325	$3,900	$450	$5,400
11	$350	$4,200	$450	$5,400
12	$375	$4,500	$450	$5,400
13	$400	$4,800	$450	$5,400
14	$425	$5,100	$450	$5,400
15	$450	$5,400	$450	$5,400
16	$475	$5,700	$450	$5,400
17	$500	$6,000	$450	$5,400
18	$525	$6,300	$450	$5,400
19	$550	$6,600	$450	$5,400
20	$575	$6,900	$450	$5,400
21	$600	$7,200	$450	$5,400
22	$625	$7,500	$450	$5,400
23	$650	$7,800	$450	$5,400
24	$675	$8,100	$450	$5,400
25	$700	$8,400	$450	$5,400
26	$725	$8,700	$450	$5,400
27	$750	$9,000	$450	$5,400
28	$775	$9,300	$450	$5,400
29	$800	$9,600	$450	$5,400
30	$825	$9,900	$450	$5,400
		$166,500		$162,000

Your Savings Plan

Year	Monthly Savings Rate (Staged)	Total Saved for Year (Monthly x 12)	Monthly Savings Rate (without Staging)	Total Saved for Year (Monthly x 12)
1	?		?	
2				
3				
4				
5				
6				
7				
8				
9				
10				
11				
12				
13				
14				
15				
16				
17				
18				
19				
20				
21				
22				
23				
24				
25				
26				
27				
28				
29				
30				
	Total		Total	

Determining your custom plan

So how much should you start saving? What length of time should you save for? Certainly those are the questions that you're thinking as you begin to explore your personal financial plan. They can be answered quickly by completing the self-assessment chart on the next page and calculating the monthly savings needed using the 5% Money Chart illustrated. The chart will help you outline a general plan to determine how much to start saving and the duration you need save for in order to achieve specific goals. It can be done in 2 steps.

Wealth Exercise #4

Step 1. Determine Your Goal

	Sample	Your Goal?
What is your goal?	Retirement	
How much time do you have until your goal?	30 Years (360 Months)	
How much total money is required to meet your goal?	$750,000	

Step 2. Calculate Your Goal

	College Funding	Automobile Purchase	Retirement
Determine Average Cost	$80,000	$17,000	$750,000
How Many Years to Goal	18	5	30
How Many Months to Goal (Years x 12)	216	60	360
Amount Needed to Save if No Interest Was Earned. (Average Cost Divided by Months to Goal)	$370 Monthly	$283 Monthly	$2,083 Monthly
Monthly Savings With Interest Earned. (Using 5% Money Chart)	$250 Monthly	$250 Monthly	$1000 Monthly

5% Money Chart

Using the Money Chart – The money chart is an easy to use guide that calculates how much money will be saved after a specific number of years. The highlighted example illustrates that a savings of $250 monthly for 5 years will result in $17,000 saved, based on a 5% interest return.

You can use the chart in three ways:

Goal Amount:
Select a goal amount from the center of the chart and simply follow it to the number of years and the monthly savings amount needed.

Amount of monthly savings:
Select an amount to save each month and follow the chart to see how much you will have saved for a specific period of time.

Number of years:
Select number of years you have until your goal, and based on the amount of money you need to save, you can follow the chart upwards to see the monthly savings required.

5% Money Chart

Monthly Savings Earning 5% Annual Interest

End of Year	Monthly Savings Amount			
	$100	$250	$500	$1,000
1	$1,227	$3,069	$6,139	$12,278
2	$2,518	$6,295	$12,590	$25,180
3	$3,875	$9,688	$19,375	$38,750
4	$5,301	$13,253	$26,505	$53,010
5	$6,800	$17,000	$34,000	$68,000
6	$8,376	$20,940	$41,880	$83,760
7	$10,032	$25,080	$50,160	$100,320
8	$11,774	$29,435	$58,870	$117,740
9	$13,604	$34,010	$68,020	$136,040
10	$15,528	$38,820	$77,640	$155,280
11	$17,550	$43,875	$87,750	$175,500
12	$19,676	$49,190	$98,380	$196,760
13	$21,910	$54,775	$109,550	$219,100
14	$24,259	$60,648	$121,295	$242,590
15	$26,728	$66,820	$133,640	$267,280
16	$29,324	$73,310	$146,620	$293,240
17	$32,052	$80,130	$160,260	$320,520
18	$34,920	$87,300	$174,600	$349,200
19	$37,934	$94,835	$189,670	$379,340
20	$41,103	$102,758	$205,515	$411,030
21	$44,434	$111,085	$222,170	$444,340
22	$47,935	$119,838	$239,675	$479,350
23	$51,615	$129,038	$258,075	$516,150
24	$55,484	$138,710	$277,420	$554,840
25	$59,550	$148,875	$297,750	$595,500
26	$63,825	$159,563	$319,125	$638,250
27	$68,318	$170,795	$341,590	$683,180
28	$73,042	$182,605	$365,210	$730,420
29	$78,006	$195,015	$390,030	$780,060
30	$83,225	$208,063	$416,125	$832,250

Road Map – Part 3: The need for consistency

Consistency is the main ingredient for success. Every discipline in life requires consistent behavior in order to succeed. Financial planning and building wealth are no different. The ability to create a financial plan and start a savings fund is fruitful only if you can consistently maintain your plan. It's the consistency of our plans that allows us to take advantage of time. Our ability to reduce expenses, evaluate opportunity costs and build wealth by saving is magnified when we consistently practice our behavior. Creating your budget and determining your starting point for savings are only the beginning. Now you must start putting your savings to work within an investment tool that can grow your savings.

Chapter 9

Simplifying your investment choices

Financial success requires the marriage of both a successful plan and the tools to fuel your plan. As we've discovered, a plan that successfully reduces your expenses will also enable you to save, while helping you maintain consistency. But once you have designed yourself a plan that achieves those objectives, it's crucial that you choose the correct tools to enable your plan. This requires an understanding of the common financial vehicles used to build wealth and the risk that comes with each choice. It's important to note that there are many choices when it comes to saving and investing your money. All of these choices offer a return on the money you invest, based upon the risk level you are willing to accept. A properly structured plan will include a variety of investments in order to achieve the best performance while spreading your risk.

What are your choices?

Saving your money is very much like being a lender. You will allow someone else to use your money, and in return they will pay you interest. The goal is to earn as much interest on your money without creating too much risk. After all, you don't want to give out your money to someone that's not able to pay you back. This is where choosing the right balance of investments is important. Rather than going into too much detail on every place you can save your money, let's look at the most common investment vehicles. Remember, you have the ability to use time to maximize your return; therefore it is always better to create a structure that gives you the most reward for the least amount of risk.

The Popular Investment Vehicles chart lists the most common investment types, and categorizes them by risk and reward. You will immediately notice that each investment type has the ability to create returns based on risk level. For example, stocks have the highest potential for return but also the highest risk. That's not to say that you shouldn't invest in stocks, but a well-structured plan starts with the proper balance of investments based upon your goals and time frame.

Interestingly enough, you probably noticed that a home is not listed in the investment chart. This goes against what many have been taught about home ownership. The simple truth is that a home is not a very good investment. It doesn't produce income and often requires the use of debt. And as many homeowners have experienced, a turn in the market can quickly destroy your equity. Our goal as a lender is to always earn an income on our investments while reducing the opportunity cost. A home does not satisfy any of our investment requirements.

Popular Investment Vehicles

Investment Type	Risk Level	Reward Level
Permanent Life Insurance Cash Value Accounts	**Low** Risk is very low due to the guarantees of many policies	**Moderate** Competitive interest rates with a variety of investment choices
Bank Savings Accounts	**Low** Strong guarantees	**Low** Low interest rates reduce the ability to substantially grow money.
Bonds	**Moderate** No guarantees	**Moderate** Interest rates can be competitive, but are tied heavily with the risk level of the bond.
Stocks	**High** No guarantees and values can vary from day-to-day	**High** Gains can be high depending on the performance of the company

Creating the right structure

Knowing how to measure the risk and reward levels of different investments will enable you to properly fund your financial plan. It's important to understand that there is no one single formula that can account for everyone's financial situation. Our goal is to establish a healthy starting point that will give the biggest opportunity to accumulate wealth. As you grow the value of your financial plan to meet your individual goals, you may find it necessary to make some adjustments.

Think of building your savings plan in the same way you would build a house (your financial house.) You would want to make sure that the foundation is solid and made up of the least amount of risk. Once we have a solid foundation, we can begin to fill our financial house with higher return and higher risk investments. This will allow you to have a savings plan that can withstand any financial storm and at the same time maximize your growth.

Cash value permanent life insurance can serve as a strong base of a financial plan due to the flexibility in which you can systematically save, earn a competitive interest rate, make withdrawals, and protect your assets. Bank savings accounts are another good base, if short-term liquidity and underlying safety is desired. Unfortunately, bank accounts don't provide above market interest rates, which in effect reduce your ability to grow your money. When using a bank account you are also faced with the challenge of having to motivate yourself to make consistent deposits. This makes saving large amounts over time more difficult, and you must constantly fight the temptation of taking unplanned withdrawals.

Mutual funds offer a great investment vehicle, allowing you to choose investment types with the ability to have systematic contributions. Bonds offer a great way to save because of their ability to give you more growth on your money, while locking your money in for a longer period of time. Unfortunately, individual bonds cannot take in systematic deposits, as all investing must be done in lump-sum. This makes consistent investing more difficult. Stocks, on the other hand, have the ability to rapidly grow your money, but have no underlying guarantees, and any short term movement in the stock market could impact your total savings goal.

Match your investment to your goal

Knowing the different choices for investments enable you

to create a plan that perfectly matches your goals with the time frame and savings amount you have available. Not only will you end up with a well balanced plan that provides the most return with the least amount of risk, but your plan will give you flexibility to achieve changing goals. This is why it's so important that the investment vehicles you choose not only earn a return, but also help you manage your goals. If your goal requires the use of staging or a long period of systematic deposits, then the investment vehicle you choose should match those needs.

If, for example, your goal required the ability to systematically save $100 monthly, then an investment in a bond would not be suitable. On the other hand, if you had a short-term goal without the need to substantially grow your money and were diligent enough to make periodic deposits, then a bank savings account might be a suitable choice. Matching the right investment vehicle with your goal will insure you success in achieving that goal. This will not only allow you to think like a lender but you will always be able to manage your money like a lender.

Chapter 10

Your private bank

Thinking and managing money like a lender allows us to create a strong financial path towards wealth. We can reduce borrowing and create a savings plan with a little preparation. And we have seen that it doesn't take more income or a high paying job to gain the same advantages used by the wealthy. The use of time combined with staging and compounding enables the creation of wealth regardless of the amount of money one starts saving. Growing wealth only requires the discipline of thinking like a lender and executing our plan. But when we think of a lender, we traditionally think of a bank. This is for a good reason. A bank is a financial vehicle that a lender can use to manage their money, and more importantly, manage the way they use their money.

If you look at a bank, and more specifically, how a lender uses a bank as a tool, you will find that they operate in two different categories. A lender uses the tool of a bank in order to raise capital, via the deposits that they take into the bank from their customers. As the lender receives money from depositors, it then offers loans back to depositors. This is the true genius behind the bank. The customers deposit their money into the bank, and the lender then converts a large portion of the depositors into borrowers. Remember...Who makes the money? The lender knows that by convincing their depositors to borrow money, they will be able to maximize their profits.

The bank becomes the perfect tool for the lender. The customer deposits their money into the bank at a much lower interest rate, and conversely borrows money at a much higher interest rate. This is a much overlooked occurrence that plagues many borrowers. It's amazing to see how many people with $50,000 in a bank savings account earning a low interest rate, will then at the same time take a car loan at a high interest rate from the same lender. In effect, they are giving the bank money and paying the bank interest to use their own money. This is a crazy occurrence, and it happens every single day.

What would I do with a bank?

Now that you know what a great tool a bank is for the lender, wouldn't it be great to own a bank? Let's assume you could start a bank. Certainly that would be an incredible way to create wealth and put you on the correct financial path. Imagine what you could do if you had your own bank? The next time you wanted to buy a car, you could loan yourself the money. If you could loan yourself the money and pay yourself interest, then borrowing would cost $0. Not only could owning a bank give you access to zero-cost loans, but what about the ability to save money in your own bank? Since you probably deposit money directly into someone else's bank today, owning your own bank would allow you to have better control on using your money for certain goals. How much money could you save if you were able to divert $100 monthly, $500 monthly, maybe $1000 monthly into your own bank?

Imagine taking the staging approach and creating a plan that would allow you to grow your savings rate each year. The benefits of owning a bank wouldn't just stop there. Assuming your bank was large enough, you would probably have experts helping you lend money to other borrowers. Now you're really making money! You could start lending (investing) your deposits, in order to build real wealth. You would be able to use time to maximize your profits. After all, your bank would probably have experts that could help you invest and participate in the gains of the stock market.

If you owned a bank, your children would certainly be appreciative. Imagine how easy it would be to save for a child's college education through your own bank. You could even give your child the ability to take a student loan from your bank at a zero interest rate. Imagine what an advantage your child would have if they could pay for college without having to pay any interest on the loan. The money they saved in interest payments would be a great down-payment on a home or even the start of a very early retirement fund. Any big purchase needing financing would be as easy as writing yourself a loan. Owning a bank would certainly seem to have its advantages. But it sounds like a fantasy. Everyone knows that it takes a lot of money to own a bank. And if you have the money to own a bank, well, then you probably don't even need a bank, right?

Certainly the idea of owning a traditional bank seems unrealistic when we think of a bank as a Brick-and-Mortar building with customers and loan officers inside. Your typical Brick-and-Mortar street corner bank is just one type of bank, one that the bank borrowers know very well. However, there is a second type of bank. It's a type of bank that can offer its owner the same privileges as a Brick-and-Mortar bank. A type of bank that can take deposits, earn interest, invest money, allow withdrawals, and even make loans. A bank that can be owned by anyone, including a parent, grandparent, business owner, even a child. This is a type of bank that is not well-known to the general population, and came into existence by accident. Like many other great inventions, this type of bank was created as a result of a financial product designed for a completely different purpose.

Where do I get a bank?

So, what is this magical bank? Where can I get it? And why doesn't everyone know about it? Those are the questions that are undoubtedly going through your mind at this moment. But before answering the first two questions of what and where, it makes sense to understand why everyone doesn't know about it. And that question can best be answered with one small phrase: "a lack of understanding from many financial professionals."

Since most financial professionals are trained by the product manufacturer to sell products based on their intended design, many professionals simply don't know that their product can function like a bank. As mentioned earlier, the ability for this financial product to work like a bank, providing many of the same functions as a bank, was not the initially intended function of the product. In fact, when this product is used to function as a bank, the product manufacturer and the financial professional do not make as much money. It's not difficult to see why a product provider would not want to promote a product in a way that does not maximize revenue.

The truly surprising answer is to the second question, where can you get this product that functions like a bank and gives its owner many of the same capabilities of a bank? It might surprise you to know that this product is available from many of the largest insurance companies in the world, and it's a product that is currently owned by many consumers. Unfortunately, most consumers don't understand that this type of bank is available to them even if they already own it. Remember, most financial professionals don't even know that these features exist.

Now that we know why and where, it might surprise you to learn that this type of bank can be owned by utilizing a permanent life insurance policy. This is surprising to most, considering the thought of insurance, especially life insurance, sends most people headed towards the closest exit. And for purposes of wealth accumulation, the protection benefits of life insurance don't interest us. It's the use of this financial product as a savings vehicle that makes it worth discussing in greater detail. Permanent life insurance plans have a number of features that make them uniquely suited for long-term savings plans. In fact, although not intentionally designed to function like a bank, these unique features allow permanent insurance policies to be used like a private bank. These features are not commonly known to the average investor and not highly advertised by the insurance companies.

Why permanent life insurance?

Insurance companies are among some of the largest financial institutions in the world. They earn their profit by managing risk and investments. One of the most widely purchased types of insurance policies is life insurance. Life insurance is sold in two forms: term and permanent. Term insurance policies charge the customers a low premium for a specific period of time, such as ten years, and then the policy must be renewed at a higher price.

Permanent policies are designed to give customers a policy that keeps their premium fixed for life. To accommodate the extended length of risk, insurance companies needed a policy that would let the customers pre-pay the premiums; so that customers wouldn't have to pay so much as they got older. To better illustrate the differences: let's suppose Johnny decided that he needed a life insurance policy to protect his family in the event he died. Johnny could purchase a term plan that guaranteed his premiums would stay the same for ten years. After ten years, Johnny would be ten years older and therefore need to pay more premiums to have the same coverage. In fact, every year Johnny's premiums could go up to the point where he could no longer afford the coverage.

Buying a ten year term policy was a good option for Johnny if he was simply looking at price, and needed the insurance for a short period of time. However, if Johnny needed the insurance for a long period of time, because of young kids or the increase in estate taxes as he got older, he might be better off purchasing a permanent insurance plan that kept his premiums from increasing in the future. The option to never have an increase in price means that Johnny would have to pay a little extra in premiums: the equivalent of pre-paying some of his premiums in the early years.

But with the need to allow customers like Johnny to pre-pay premiums, insurance companies had to create an account to hold the customers' extra premiums. This account is called the policy cash value account, and just like any account that holds money, the cash value account earns interest. Since the primary purpose of the cash account is to help pay future premiums, the insurance company is motivated to see the money grow. This is why many insurance companies credit far better interest rates to account values than you could earn at your local bank. After all, they are going to get that money back in future premiums.

Over-funding the account value

But what if you over-funded the account value in order to take advantage of the higher interest rates? Instead of using the account just to hold future premiums, you could use it to accumulate money while earning competitive interest. This is exactly what many wealthy people figured out as the popularity of cash value accounts grew among the rich. In fact, so many wealthy people began putting huge amounts of money into permanent insurance cash accounts that in 1987, the IRS began restricting the amount of money that could be accumulated in these plans. This spelled bad news for many wealthy investors seeking to take advantage of the account value, but the restrictions had little impact on the average American. And even with the restrictions in place, many wealthy investors continue to maximize the amount of savings they put into cash value accounts today. The account value is the jewel of a permanent insurance policy. Your ability to accumulate wealth and manage your money is all centered on these accounts.

Chapter 11

Permanent life insurance will work for you

Since an insurance company is not a bank, and their primary role has nothing to do with inducing you to become a borrower, they are the perfect institution for you to use to administrate your own bank. Unlike a traditional Brick-and-Mortar bank that is incentivized to keep you a borrower, the insurance company would rather see you grow your investment. By utilizing the services through the policy and making deposits into the policy account value, you are in essence lending the insurance company money in return for an interest rate.

Many permanent life insurance plans are designed with an abundance of flexibility. Not only do they offer all the functions of a bank, but the administrative capabilities of these plans allow an amazing amount of flexibility in the way deposits and withdrawals are taken. Deposits can be made with lump sums, level periodic deposits, increasing (staged) deposits, and just about any other way you can think of. As flexible as these policies are to receiving deposits, they are equally flexible in the way you can access your money. Most policies can be designed to pay out an income, allow periodic withdrawals, and even have the flexibility to let you loan yourself money. And finally, if all of that weren't enough, if the owner wanted to use the policy for a retirement fund, he could take out loans tax-free, and never pay them back. Later in the book, we will discuss in greater detail how you can use these features. Many modern plans also have the capability of allowing the owner to be involved in investment decisions including what stock market indexes they wish to follow. They allow the owner to choose the level of return on their investments based upon their risk tolerance.

Sign me up!

So how does it all get put together? Simply stated, by purchasing a permanent life insurance policy you are purchasing life insurance *plus* an account that will hold all your premium deposits. The portion of premiums not needed to cover the insurance cost is diverted into an account earning interest. As that account value builds in size, you can use that money to take withdrawals and/or loans. Remember, the money in your permanent policy cash value account is your money. The cash account is simply an account that holds the money you pay into the policy, until it is needed in the future. And although there are obvious advantages for anyone with dependents to use life insurance as a savings tool, anyone seeking to accumulate wealth can use these tools, regardless of the need for insurance protection.

Wealth through deposits

The flexibility of deposits is a powerful tool of permanent insurance. Owners have the ability to grow their policy cash account with a slew of choices: systematic deposits, lump sum deposits, and even staged deposits. It is the capability of automatic deposits that allow owners to systematically build wealth in their policy account. Automatic monthly deposits are such a powerful tool for savings because they allow you to set a monthly budget for savings, and the insurance company will automatically deduct that savings amount from your checking accounts. If you are a government worker, in the military, postal worker, teacher, or part of some other sponsored employee programs, then the insurance company can deduct the premiums directly from your paycheck.

Make yourself a loan

Loan features on permanent insurance plans can create an amazing opportunity for owners to fund life's events. Rather than forcing policy holders to withdrawal money from their cash account, insurance companies would rather you loan yourself the money from your cash account, knowing that you will pay yourself back, thereby keeping the money invested with them. Remember, insurance companies are not banks and are not financially motivated to make you a borrower. They would rather you keep the money in the account, so that they can retain you as an insurance customer.

If you have $10,000 in your cash value account, you can simply loan yourself a portion of your money – let's say $6,000 – to remodel your bathroom. As you pay your loan back, you are simply repaying yourself as this money goes back into your cash value account.

Whether it's for the purchase of an automobile, down payment on a home, college funding, or retirement needs, a loan allows you to receive money from the policy cash value, and then decide on the re-payment schedule that fits best. The insurance company will administrate the re-payments and any payment you make will go back into your cash account.

What's even more impressive is that although money has been loaned out of the cash value account of the policy, the policy will continue to earn interest as if the money had never been taken out. This is an amazingly powerful feature because it does not penalize you for borrowing your own money. You will be hard-pressed to find a traditional bank that will loan you money and continue to pay interest on the money as if it were still deposited in your account. That is exactly what your permanent insurance bank can do.

Let's use Adam, the banker's son, as an example. Although Adam is single and has no dependents, he realizes the need to begin saving for his future. He would like to purchase a new car in the next five years, and dreams of an early retirement at age 55. And although he has a work-sponsored retirement plan, Adam decides to purchase a permanent life insurance policy to assist him in his savings goals. He begins a systematic savings plan that automatically deposits money into his new policy each month. After five years of automatic deposits and interest accumulation, he will have $20,000 of cash value. Once he has saved enough money for his car, he will take a loan from his policy cash value in order to purchase a new car, rather than going to the local bank. Since he took a loan from his policy, he has decided to pay himself back over a six year period.

Since Adam has borrowed his own money, not withdrawn it, the $20,000 that he has saved is still in his account earning interest while he continues to save for retirement. Twenty years later, Adam has long ago repaid his loan, and has accumulated enough money for his retirement. Now Adam's biggest decision is how much monthly income he wants to pay himself from his cash value account.

Adam chose to save using a permanent insurance plan, not because he needed the life insurance protection, but because he wanted the flexibility that the policy account offered. The features available using permanent insurance as a savings vehicle are unmatched by any other investment type. No other individual investment accounts including stocks, bonds, bank accounts or bank certificates of deposits enable an investor to earn interest while having features such as withdrawals, zero cost loans, and asset protection from the life insurance benefits. Most other investments only reward savings with an interest rate. And while there are many good options for an investor to save money, permanent insurance is the only option that allows you to stop acting like a borrower and start saving like a lender.

Tax-deferred growth

One of the most compelling advantages for using a permanent insurance plan as a private bank is the accumulation of growth on a tax-deferred basis. Unlike non-IRA deposits that are made at other financial institutions such as a bank, the interest that is earned in a permanent insurance plan is not taxed until the money is withdrawn. This creates a huge growth advantage due to the compounding effect.

For example, if you were to deposit $1000 in a regular bank savings account earning 4% interest, you would earn $40 annually. However, that $40 you earn is now subject to income taxes. After taxes that $40 might now only be worth $28. What's worse, the effects of compounding have been reduced because only $28 will be working to earn interest for you. When properly structured, money earned in a permanent insurance plan *will not* be subject to income taxes; allowing you to grow *all* of the money you earned. The taxes are deferred until you withdrawal the money from the policy.

Anyone can start at any time

The ability to own your own bank and become your own lender is available now. Through the unique design of permanent insurance policies, insurance companies have created the perfect private bank. Permanent insurance policies have been used by the wealthy for many years. It is an investment vehicle that can be used at any time by anyone, regardless of the need for insurance protection. And although many of the benefits of the permanent insurance bank have been created to enhance the value for wealthy investors, anyone can participate. Owning your own bank and taking the steps to secure your financial goals requires little more than developing and implementing your financial plan.

Now you're thinking like a Lender!

Chapter 12

Planning for retirement

Retirement planning is one of the most talked about financial topics. You are hard-pressed to turn on any financial television program or read a money magazine without mention of retirement. Yet, most of us are either unprepared for retirement or don't know where to start. A survey conducted by the Employee Benefit Research Institute showed that over 43% of Americans had less than $10,000 in savings. With that statistic in mind, it's not surprising that fewer than 40% of Americans are saving for retirement outside of work. If you're like most Americans, the thought of retirement savings crosses your mind from time to time, but the act of implementing a consistent retirement plan keeps getting pushed into the future.

The most challenging obstacle we face in retirement planning is our inability to think far enough ahead. Our need to satisfy upcoming expenses, such as a mortgage, car payment and credit cards, have a dampening effect on our excitement to save for events that may not occur for twenty, thirty, even forty years. Unfortunately, our retirement needs will make up the greatest expense of our lives. In retirement years, the need for income is amplified by our need for medicines, health care, and entertainment. After all, why retire if you can't enjoy the time off?

As of 2009, the average life expectancy in the United States was just over 79. That life expectancy increases each decade as medicine and healthcare improvements are made. With an average retirement age of 65, most Americans must anticipate the need for retirement funds to last over 15 years. That is 15 years of income that you must replace in order to live without a job. To better understand how much money is needed to retire, take your total earnings over the last 15 years of work and add them up. Do you have that much saved for retirement today? Probably not. And if you are thinking that it's a big number, you're right.

Imagine if Adam were making $50,000 a year and he wanted to retire at age 65. In order to retire without fear of running out of money, he must save at least $750,000 ($50,000 x 15 years during retirement.) Without factoring in interest or inflation, Adam would have to save ALL of his income for the last 15 years of his working life in order to have enough saved. Even if Adam started saving thirty years before retirement, he would still have to save half of everything he makes, in order to save enough ($25,000 x 30 = $750,000). Saving for retirement requires the acceptance that we must start planning and saving as early as possible. Time can be either our ally or our enemy, and no one can afford to waste any of it.

A quick thought on taxes

Understanding how much is needed to save for retirement allows us to build a proper retirement plan. But the decision of which savings tool to use for retirement requires an understanding of how money is affected by taxes. This is easy to understand in that there are three ways your money is taxed when it comes to retirement savings.

1. You pay income taxes when you make your money or;
2. You might pay income taxes when you withdrawal your money and you also;
3. Pay income taxes when your money makes you money.

For example, if you get paid $50,000 from work, you understand that $15,000 gets paid to Uncle Sam Tax Collector. If you put $1000 in the bank and earn $50, then your $50 earnings also get taxed.

In saving for retirement it's important to choose a plan that reduces the taxes paid. After all, no one wants to give hard-earned money away. The first tax, the tax paid on income from our job, will be paid no matter what – but we can choose when to pay taxes when selecting a retirement plan. We can choose a plan that lets us pay our taxes as we earn our money, or in the case of a qualified retirement plan such as a 401K or an IRA, we can pay our taxes after we retire, and start withdrawing money.

The third tax that we pay, the tax on our interest earnings, can greatly affect how much we are able to save. By paying taxes every year as we earn interest, we are reducing the amount of savings that we have working for us.

The solution to this tax is called tax deferral. Tax deferral offered by some investment products allows all the interest earnings to skip taxation until a future point in time. Deferring taxes is obviously an advantage, but as with most other things relating to taxes, the day will come when Uncle Sam must be paid.

The power of tax deferral

Permanent life insurance has the added benefit of allowing all interest accumulation in the cash account to be tax-deferred. This means that all of the earnings that build up in the account will remain in the account to make more money. The earnings are never eroded by income taxes, and you only pay income taxes on the earnings when you take the money out. This is very advantageous for retirement planning. And since you are depositing money in the permanent policy after you have already paid taxes, you will only be taxed on the interest when you take the money out, not on the full amount withdrawn. For example, if you are withdrawing $50,000 per year for retirement and $8,000 of the $50,000 was interest you earned, then you will only pay taxes on $8,000. A 401K or traditional IRA, however, would tax you on the full $50,000. Imagine what a dent that would do to your retirement income.

Give yourself a tax-free retirement

The flexibility of permanent insurance as a private bank does not stop with withdrawals, but includes the policy's unique ability to let you loan yourself money. That's right, rather than taking a withdrawal for retirement, you can loan yourself money out of your cash account. Remember, your permanent policy is like a bank. At any time you can loan yourself a portion of your money. Since loans are not considered withdrawals, all loans are tax-free, even the interest earned is loaned tax-free. This is an advantage that no other savings vehicle offers.

How is this possible? Loans are tax-free because they are not considered income by Uncle Sam. Think of the last loan you applied for. Whether it was a mortgage or car loan, there were no income taxes to be paid on the money you received. Loans are always tax-free because eventually you will pay back the loan with money that has been taxed (your income-taxed earnings.) As long as your permanent insurance policy stays in force, the loan you make yourself from your policy account value will be eventually repaid upon your death, out of your life insurance death benefit. That means that you can give yourself a tax-free loan from your policy, and never be required to pay yourself back. The policy's life insurance benefit will make everything whole at the end. There is no other savings product that can do all of this.

The key to having a tax-free retirement is making sure that your policy stays in force. If your policy runs out of money and lapses, then the loans are considered withdrawals and taxes on the interest will be due. To prevent this, many modern permanent policies have built in no-lapse features that will prevent the policy from lapsing. These features guarantee that your policy will always have enough money in the account value to stay in force. If you are planning on using loans for retirement planning, this is a very important feature to have.

401K's, IRA, permanent insurance, which is best?

Choosing the right vehicle to fund a savings plan can be a confusing task. Each vehicle has advantages and disadvantages based on the time frame and flexibility requirements of your retirement goal. As discussed, permanent life insurance has a number of features that enhance its value as retirement savings plan. But what about all the other options? How do they compare with permanent insurance?

A 401K is an employer-sponsored plan that allows you to contribute money to your account before income taxes are paid. This does not mean that you never have to pay taxes; instead the taxes are paid when you take the money out at retirement. The disadvantage of this approach is that rather than paying taxes on a small amount going in (before you start earning interest) to the plan, your are waiting to then pay taxes on a larger amount (after you have grown your money) when you take the money out. Remember the Doubling Money rule. If you save $1,000 today at 5%, it will grow to over $4,400 over thirty years. Simply put, would you rather pay taxes on $1,000 today or on $4,400 in 30 years? It is more cost effective to pay taxes on your money before it starts growing.

The ability to take early withdrawals is also more difficult with a 401K plan. Any withdrawals prior to age 59 ½ are subject to a 10% penalty in addition to income taxes. This in effect locks your money in without any flexibility and eliminates this plan type if you're planning an early retirement prior to age 59 ½. And unlike permanent life insurance plans, 401K's do not allow loans, eliminating your ability to take money out without paying taxes. As with any IRS-sponsored plan, 401K's have limited contribution amounts, making it difficult to achieve many retirement goals.

An IRA, on the other hand, allows you to choose between two plans. A traditional IRA will tax your money when you take it out, and a Roth IRA will let you pay taxes before you put the money in. And although IRA's have some tax flexibility, they don't allow money to be withdrawn before age 59 ½, without the 10% penalty. And like the 401K, the inability to take loans limits access to your money.

Permanent insurance has the unique ability to take in systematic deposits, earn a competitive interest, allow withdrawals at any time, and use loans in order to reduce the tax burden. These vehicles also have a great deal of flexibility in the amount that can be contributed into the plan, enabling you to satisfy almost any retirement goal. And let's not forget the added benefit that if your retirement plan is being funded for both you and a spouse, the life insurance death benefit guarantees that your spouse will have a retirement fund in the event of a death.

When comparing the different types of retirement vehicles it is important to evaluate whether you may need to take early withdrawals, plan for an early retirement, insure that a spouse has guaranteed retirement funds in the event of your death or require reducing your overall tax burden. A comparison of the features and benefit of each plan type is made in the following chart. The Emergency Early Withdrawal chart illustrates the effect of penalties and taxes on qualified 401K and IRA plans.

Emergency Early Withdrawal
(Withdrawals prior to age 59 ½)

	Johnny using a 401K / Traditional IRA	Adam using Permanent Life Insurance
Emergency Withdrawal at Age 55	$50,000	$50,000
Amount Received After Penalties and Taxes	$31,000 (10% penalty and income taxes)	$50,000 (no penalties or taxes using loan)

Notice the effects of taxes on the following Retirement Planning Comparison chart. Using Johnny and Adam as an example, we can see that both have saved $750,000. Assuming Johnny was 59 ½ and they each began taking out $50,000 over the course of 15 years, Johnny would be left with $36,000 after taxes. On the other hand, by utilizing the tax-free loan feature of his permanent life insurance plan, Adam would pay $0 taxes and keep his full $50,000.

Retirement Planning Comparison

	Johnny using a 401K / Traditional IRA	Adam using Permanent Life Insurance
Total Saved at Retirement	**$750,000**	**$750,000**
Retirement Income Withdrawn Over 15 years	$50,000	$50,000
Taxes Paid (28% bracket)	$14,000	$0 (using loans)
After tax retirement income	$36,000	$55,000
Total Income Received Over 15 Years	**$540,000**	**$750,000**
Tax-deferred Interest Accumulation	YES	YES
Allow for Penalty-free Early Withdrawals	NO	YES
Allows Loans	NO	YES

Reaching your retirement goal

Since it's highly unlikely that we can save 100% or even 50% of what we make in order to fund a retirement plan, we must use every tool available to maximize our savings. A proper retirement plan will make use of time, staging our savings, interest earnings, and any tax incentives we can get. By using all of the tools we have learned we can begin to structure a proper retirement savings plan.

Using our prior example; Adam at age 35 decides he would like to retire at age 65, creating the need to replace his $50,000 after-tax annual income. That gives Adam 30 years to save. Since he calculates that his average life expectancy will be age 80, he will need a minimum of 15 years income replacement. Adam calculates his retirement savings needs to be $750,000 (15 years multiplied by $50,000). Using the 5% Money Chart, he determines that he will need to save almost $1000 monthly.

At the present time, this is more than he can afford so he decides to commit himself to a staged savings plan. Using the Staged 5% Money Chart, Adam determines that he can afford to start saving $500 monthly while increasing his monthly savings each year by $50 per month. This will allow him to achieve his retirement goal with over $854,000 saved in thirty years.

Adam's Retirement Plan

	Retirement
Determine Goal	$750,000
How Many Years to Goal	30
How Many Months to Goal (years x 12)	360
Monthly Savings with Interest Earned. (Using 5% Money Chart)	$1000 Monthly
Monthly Savings Using Staging. (Using 5% Staging Money Chart)	$500 Monthly

5% Staged Money Chart

	Monthly Savings with Staging and 5% Annual Interest			
End of Year	$100 Monthly with $10 Annual Increases	$250 Monthly with $25 Annual Increases	$500 Monthly with $50 Annual Increases	$1000 Monthly with $100 Annual Increases
1	$1,227	$3,069	$6,139	$12,278
2	$2,638	$6,596	$13,190	$26,381
3	$4,242	$10,606	$21,212	$42,424
4	$6,050	$15,125	$30,248	$60,496
5	$8,070	$20,175	$40,349	$80,698
6	$10,314	$25,785	$51,569	$103,138
7	$12,793	$31,983	$63,964	$127,927
8	$15,518	$38,796	$77,591	$155,183
9	$18,503	$46,258	$92,514	$185,028
10	$21,759	$54,399	$108,796	$217,592
11	$25,301	$63,254	$126,506	$253,012
12	$29,143	$72,858	$145,715	$291,429
13	$33,299	$83,250	$166,497	$332,995
14	$37,787	$94,467	$188,933	$377,866
15	$42,621	$106,553	$213,103	$426,207
16	$47,819	$119,549	$239,096	$478,192
17	$53,400	$133,502	$267,002	$534,004
18	$59,383	$148,459	$296,917	$593,833
19	$65,788	$164,471	$328,940	$657,881
20	$72,636	$181,591	$363,179	$726,358
21	$79,949	$199,873	$399,743	$799,486
22	$87,750	$219,376	$438,748	$877,497
23	$96,064	$240,160	$480,318	$960,636
24	$104,916	$262,291	$524,579	$1,049,159
25	$114,333	$285,835	$571,667	$1,143,335
26	$124,345	$310,863	$621,723	$1,243,446
27	$134,979	$337,449	$674,895	$1,349,791
28	$146,268	$365,672	$731,340	$1,462,679
29	$158,244	$395,612	$791,220	$1,582,439
30	$170,941	$427,356	$854,707	$1,709,414

Combining all of your retirement tools

By combining all of the tools Adam has learned, he is able to construct a retirement plan that works within his budget. He uses staging in order to grow his funds, and utilizes a permanent insurance plan so that he doesn't have to pay income taxes on the interest he accumulates. At retirement, Adam can choose whether he wants to withdrawal his money entirely or take a tax-free retirement, based on his current tax rate. Adam's plan has given him a true road map for success.

Your retirement planning is no different than Adam's. It all begins with determining a goal, and calculating the time available to reach your goal. Using the 5% Money Chart or the 5% Staged Money Chart, complete the following exercise and create your retirement plan.

Wealth Exercise #5

	Retirement
Determine Goal	$_____
How Many Years to Goal	_____
How Many Months to Goal (Years x 12)	_____
Monthly Savings with Interest Earned (Using 5% Money Chart)	$_____ Monthly
Monthly savings using staging (Using 5% Staging Money Chart)	$_____ Monthly

Chapter 13

College savings planning

There are many uses for your permanent life insurance savings vehicle. The flexibility of loans enables you to fund a variety of savings goals requiring the use of your money at a predetermined time. Among one of the best uses for a permanent insurance plan is college savings. College savings planning requires us to determine the future cost of education, length of education, and amount we can budget for our savings. We must also choose a savings vehicle that not only allows for flexibility in the way we take out money, but guarantees that our savings goal will be reached even upon our death. It is vitally important that we insure our children's education, even if we are no longer around to save for them. As we saw with Adam, the ability to give a child a cost-free education is invaluable to their financial future.

According to the National Center for Education, in 2008 the average annual cost (including tuition and expenses) of a four year public college education was just shy of $20,000 annually. A private college four-year education shot up to over $35,000 annually. That means that the total cost for a student to attend college over a four-year period currently ranges between $80,000 and $140,000. What's more disturbing is a 2008 study conducted by the U.S. Department of Education showed the average College Graduate graduating with $23,000 in student loans. This is in addition to the average credit card balance held by graduating students of over $8,200. All of this added together means that the children in America graduate from college and start their financial lives with an average of over $31,000 of debt.

It's no surprise that many Americans simply cannot get ahead of their debt. Not only do young Americans have to compete in an increasingly competitive world of fewer jobs, but they must start their futures having to play financial catch-up. This is not the dream of parents, and certainly not the American ideal of having your child live a better life than you lived. Fortunately, your child's financial future does not have to have such a rocky start. Saving for a college fund is made simple with a few planning tools. Since most parents have the opportunity of time, more specifically up to eighteen years, until their child must go to college, saving for college can be easily budgeted.

Predict the future cost

Having a flexible tool for college savings is only as valuable as our ability to properly determine a savings goal. This becomes more difficult given the need to plan for a seemingly unknown future cost. This is why before planning a college budget, it's important to evaluate the type of school your child will most probably attend. Since the cost of private schools vary so much from public schools it's important to select the type of school that you would want your child to attend. This will help you determine the correct college savings goal.

Knowing the current cost of a private or public college will not do much good if your child will be attending in 18 years. After all, there are very few items that have not increased in cost over the last 18 years and college tuition is certainly not one of them. A study conducted using college tuitions from 1958 to 2005, show the average college tuition increased at a rate of about 1.3x inflation or roughly 5% per year. The easiest way to predict the future cost of college tuition is by simply using the College Inflation Calculator, which is based on the average increase of 5% annually.

College Inflation Calculator

Years Until Tuition	Inflation Factor	Example per $1000 of Current Tuition
5	1.3	$1000 x 1.3 = $1300 Cost in 5 years
10	1.6	$1000 x 1.6 = $1600 Cost in 10 years
15	2.1	$1000 x 2.1 = $2100 Cost in 15 years
18	2.4	$1000 x 2.4 = $2400 Cost in 18 years

2010 Cost of Public College = $20,000

2010 Cost of Private College = $35,000

Calculate your savings plan

Calculating a savings goal is easy once a school type is determined, and an estimate of the future cost is calculated. If we were to plan a college savings for a three year old girl, using the College Inflation calculator, we could determine that over the next fifteen years the cost of an education would double. If the average expense for a public college is $20,000 annually, then in fifteen years the average expense will be approximately $42,000 ($20,000 x 2.1) We would be required to save a total of $168,000 ($42,000 x 4 years) in order to fund a four year degree.

Using our 5% Money Charts we can see that we must save approximately $600 monthly or with the use of a staging program we can start by saving $400 monthly.

	College Savings
Determine Goal	$168,000
How Many Years to Goal	15
How Many Months to Goal (years x 12)	180
Monthly Savings with Interest Earned. (Using 5% Money Chart)	Aprox. $600 Monthly
Monthly Savings Using Staging (Using 5% Staging Money Chart)	Aprox. $400 Monthly

Wealth Exercise #6:

Plan your child's college fund in 3 quick steps.

  1. **Decide on a college type?**
      a. Private =$35,000 annually
      b. Public=$20,000 annually

  2. **Determine the future cost?**

Years to College	Inflation Factor Used	Current Tuition per Year x 4	Future Tuition (Inflation Factor x Current Tuition)

  3. **Calculate your savings**

	College Savings
Determine Goal	$_____
How Many Years to Goal	_____
How Many Months to Goal (Years x 12)	____
Monthly Savings with Interest Earned (Using 5% Money Chart)	$_____
Monthly Savings Using Staging (Using 5% Staging Money Chart)	$_____

Giving your child a zero-cost student loan

In the beginning of the book we learned how Adam was able to attend college without accumulating debt from interest payments. Rather than taking a traditional student loan, like his friend Johnny, Adam was able to borrow money from his father, the banker. As Adam paid back the money he borrowed from his father, Adam was allowed to keep the interest that would have been due on a traditional student loan. This put him in a great financial position and well ahead of his friend Johnny. What was not told in the story is that Adam's father had set up a college savings plan using a permanent life insurance policy.

When it was time for Adam to attend school, his father simply took a loan from his policy cash value. Once Adam graduated from school, he began paying his father back the loan. Since Adam did not have to pay any interest, he was able to pay back the loan without accumulating more debt. After graduating college, Adam was in a much better financial position than Johnny, and Adam's father had not lost any money from his savings.

Protecting your child's college fund

Using permanent life insurance as a vehicle to save for a child's college education is unmatched by any other savings product. Not only does the permanent insurance plan allow you to systematically make monthly deposits in order to reach your goal, but it then has the flexibility of allowing loans when the money is needed. By utilizing loans, the policy will remain in force, and the account value will continue to earn interest. Not only does the permanent policy help you administrate a savings plan, but the fact that it also has life insurance protection guarantees that your child will continue to have college funds, if you were to die. No other savings product has such a wide range of benefit for college funding.

Chapter 14

Gifting a life-time savings plan

The impact of our financial decisions can be seen throughout our lives. Our ability to reshape our thinking, and use the tools we have learned enables us to forge a better path for ourselves. But what about those closest to us? How can we use our newly acquired financial skills to enable our children and grandchildren to have a better life? This is the gift Adam's dad gave him, and the ultimate gift we can give to others. It is this idea, the American dream, to enable each successive generation to live a better life. This dream has been the bedrock of American growth and ingenuity. It has enabled the United States to become the world's largest economic power.

That is why it is so surprising when the latest polls and surveys are conducted among Americans. A recent Gallup Poll was conducted asking parents if they thought their children would have a better life than they do. A staggering 55% said that they didn't believe their children would have a better life. In another survey, fewer than 4 in 10 people in high income families thought their children would have more opportunities. In yet another telephone survey, conducted by Rasmussen, only 30% of Americans surveyed believed that the quality of life was better now than it had been for the prior generation.

Helping our children's future

The American dream of enabling our future generations does not come for free. The price that must be paid by current generations includes teaching our children the tools for proper financial planning, and establishing a plan early in their lives. At one time, it was common practice for a parent to open their child a savings account. Each week, the parent would teach their child the valuable lessons of saving by visiting the bank, and helping them deposit a portion of their allowance into savings. These fundamental exercises helped shape the financial futures of many children. In order to maximize the opportunities in life, it is imperative that we continue to show children the proper financial ways early in their lives.

The ultimate gift

Every loving parent or grandparent wants to expand the opportunities of their children. What if you could not only expand their opportunities, but also give them a financial head start that would last them the rest of their lives? Imagine if your parents had given you a college fund, a down-payment for your first home, and even planned a retirement fund while you were just a baby. We understand the value of time and have seen how money grows using the 5% money charts, so just imagine how much farther along you would be in your financial planning if a retirement fund had been started at your birth. That would be a whole 65 years of savings.

Certainly the opportunities you have in life would be much greater had you received the gift of a life-time savings plan from your parents. What if you could give your children this amazing gift and it did not have to cost much extra from your monthly budget? Let's look at Adam's father, from earlier in this book. We know that Adam's father helped Adam with college, and put Adam on a lifelong financial course that made him better off financially than Johnny. Suppose Adam's father started saving $100 monthly at Adam's birth, and continued to save the same $100 until Adam was twenty. By using our 5% Money Chart, we know that Adam would have over $41,000 when he is twenty. Not only would $41,000 give Adam a nice head start in life, but imagine if Adam kept that money in savings until he was sixty-five. Assuming he never added to the money, at age sixty-five he would have over $328,000. The chart below illustrates how this works.

Amount Saved	Rule of 72, Money Doubled Every 14 Years
Adam's Dad Saves $100 Monthly for 20 Years	Birth to Age 20
$41,000	Age 20
$82,000	14 Years Later, Age 34
$164,000	28 Year Later, Age 48
$328,000	42 Years Later, Age 62

Gifting a Permanent Insurance Plan

Suppose Adam's father had used a permanent life insurance policy as the vehicle to fund the life-time savings plan and made Adam the owner at birth. Remember, anyone can own a permanent life plan at anytime. Once Adam turned eighteen and needed to go to college, he could take a loan from his permanent policy cash value account instead of a student loan. We know from learning about permanent life policies that by taking a loan, the account value will continue to earn interest during the loan period. Once Adam repaid the loan, he would still have all the money in his cash value account.

Now imagine if a few years later, Adam wanted to buy his first home. He could then take a loan from his cash value account for the down payment. Adam could then set up a payment plan to pay the loan back to his cash value account over a period of time that fit his budget. Finally, when Adam is ready to retire, he would have a great retirement supplement in his cash value account. Remember, every time Adam needed money he was able to give himself a loan and pay himself back. All of this flexibility was gifted to Adam by his dad for very little money. It's easy to see how our story with Johnny and Adam turned out the way it did.

Permanent life insurance serves as a great vehicle to give a child the gift of a life-time savings plan. The flexibility of loans and how loans can be used to fund life's event are impressive. With the example given above, we used a monthly savings amount of $100. Imagine the effects of increasing that amount to $200, $300, even $500 monthly. It is not unreasonable to think that a parent could give their child the gift of a multi-million dollar retirement. The ability to gift a child time has a multiplying effect on the money you put into the plan. Remember the value of time. It is the combination of money and time that is really being gifted to the child.

Avoiding gift taxes

Gifting a child a Life-Time Savings Plan using a permanent life insurance policy also has the unique advantages of avoiding gift taxes and deferring taxes on earnings. The first tax that is avoided is the gifting tax, since the amount being saved in the policy falls well short of the IRS Gifting Tax limits. Explained in more detail; the gifting tax is a tax that is paid depending on your estate situation, and as of 2011, on any gifts exceeding $13,000. Now, that may seem like a limit that you would never exceed, but remember how much money Adam's cash account had saved over the course of twenty, even forty years. If you had the financial ability to wait and simply gift a child or grandchild a large lump-sum or the equivalent amount of Adam's cash account, you would surely be subject to gift taxes. By using systematic deposit into a plan over a period of years, the gift tax limits are never exceeded and the final value of the gift to the child is amplified by time and interest earnings.

The second tax advantage of using a permanent life insurance plan as a savings vehicle is the deferral of taxes on interest earnings. Earlier in the book, we discussed the advantages of tax-deferred savings and how taxes reduce the earning power of money. In a life-time savings plan where time is a large part of the growth formula, the need to defer taxes becomes magnified. After all, what good is having the advantage of time if your child has to pay taxes on the earnings each year? And if you are thinking that a low amount like $100 monthly saved would not produce a big tax burden, remember that after twenty years the amount became $41,000. Although the contributions are small, the ultimate value of the cash account can grow very large. It's the amount that the money grows into that needs to be protected from taxes.

Who can gift

The gift of a life-time savings plan can be made at anytime by anyone. Gifting a child is most common among parents and grandparents, wanting to better their child's future. A permanent life insurance plan containing a cash account can be purchased for any age child in order to fund a life-time savings plan. And with the ability to give systematic deposits, rather than giving a child the extra video game or stocking stuffer during the holidays, a life time gift can be made. However, it's important to remember that the real gift being made is a combination of money and time. This is why it is imperative that the gift-giver maintains a consistent plan of deposits for a period of no less than ten years. This will allow the funds to reach a large enough size to begin creating significant earnings from interest. And although the child will not appreciate the gift when she is young, when she is off to college or starting her adulthood, she will be reminded of this gift for the rest of her life.

Chapter 15

Wrapping it all up

The story of Johnny and Adam serves as a reminder that the way we think about our money has as much impact on our financial wellbeing as the way we spend it. How we think about time effects our ability to make the most of our money. And understanding the value of time lets us better evaluate the cost of everything we own, and more importantly the opportunity cost of everything we own. These fundamental differences in the way Johnny and Adam approached buying a home, financing a car, savings for retirement, and many other financial decisions made a huge impact on the way each was able to live.

Adam was always able to drive a better car, spend less money for a home, save for an early retirement, all while earning the same income as Johnny. But the lessons learned by Adam, through his father, the banker, are not exclusive to Adam. The ability to change behaviors in order to put oneself on the proper financial path is available anytime, regardless of income or profession. Adam's father knew this as he prepared his son for life, all starting with something as simple as a student loan. Adam was then able to take those lessons learned and apply them to his own son as he began a college savings plan. And with the information Johnny had now learned from his lifelong friend Adam, he began to re-chart his own financial path.

Lessons learned by Johnny...

1. Consider the cost not the price;
2. Never forget the opportunity cost of an item;
3. Always value time;
4. Never procrastinate planning for your goal;
5. Start a life-time savings plan today;
6. Give your children and grandchildren a lifetime gift.

Investment
And
Goal Planning Charts

How to use the 5% Money Charts

Using the Money Chart – The money chart is an easy to use guide that calculates how much money will be saved after a specific number of years. The highlighted example illustrates that a savings of $250 monthly for 5 years will result in $17,000 saved, based on a 5% interest return.

You can use the chart in three ways:

Goal Amount:
Select a goal amount from the center of the chart and simply follow it to the number of years and the monthly savings amount needed.

Amount of monthly savings:
Select an amount to save each month and follow the chart to see how much you will have saved for a specific period of time.

Number of years:
Select the number of years you have until your goal, and based on the amount of money you need to save, you can follow the chart up to see the monthly savings required.

5% Money Chart

Monthly Savings Earning 5% Annual Interest

End of Year	Monthly Savings Amount			
	$100	$250	$500	$1,000
1	$1,227	$3,069	$6,139	$12,278
2	$2,518	$6,295	$12,590	$25,180
3	$3,875	$9,688	$19,375	$38,750
4	$5,301	$13,253	$26,505	$53,010
5	$6,800	$17,000	$34,000	$68,000
6	$8,376	$20,940	$41,880	$83,760
7	$10,032	$25,080	$50,160	$100,320
8	$11,774	$29,435	$58,870	$117,740
9	$13,604	$34,010	$68,020	$136,040
10	$15,528	$38,820	$77,640	$155,280
11	$17,550	$43,875	$87,750	$175,500
12	$19,676	$49,190	$98,380	$196,760
13	$21,910	$54,775	$109,550	$219,100
14	$24,259	$60,648	$121,295	$242,590
15	$26,728	$66,820	$133,640	$267,280
16	$29,324	$73,310	$146,620	$293,240
17	$32,052	$80,130	$160,260	$320,520
18	$34,920	$87,300	$174,600	$349,200
19	$37,934	$94,835	$189,670	$379,340
20	$41,103	$102,758	$205,515	$411,030
21	$44,434	$111,085	$222,170	$444,340
22	$47,935	$119,838	$239,675	$479,350
23	$51,615	$129,038	$258,075	$516,150
24	$55,484	$138,710	$277,420	$554,840
25	$59,550	$148,875	$297,750	$595,500
26	$63,825	$159,563	$319,125	$638,250
27	$68,318	$170,795	$341,590	$683,180
28	$73,042	$182,605	$365,210	$730,420
29	$78,006	$195,015	$390,030	$780,060
30	$83,225	$208,063	$416,125	$832,250

5% Staged Money Chart

	Monthly Savings with Staging and 5% Annual Interest			
End of Year	$100 Monthly with $10 Annual Increases	$250 Monthly with $25 Annual Increases	$500 Monthly with $50 Annual Increases	$1000 Monthly with $100 Annual Increases
1	$1,227	$3,069	$6,139	$12,278
2	$2,638	$6,596	$13,190	$26,381
3	$4,242	$10,606	$21,212	$42,424
4	$6,050	$15,125	$30,248	$60,496
5	$8,070	$20,175	$40,349	$80,698
6	$10,314	$25,785	$51,569	$103,138
7	$12,793	$31,983	$63,964	$127,927
8	$15,518	$38,796	$77,591	$155,183
9	$18,503	$46,258	$92,514	$185,028
10	$21,759	$54,399	$108,796	$217,592
11	$25,301	$63,254	$126,506	$253,012
12	$29,143	$72,858	$145,715	$291,429
13	$33,299	$83,250	$166,497	$332,995
14	$37,787	$94,467	$188,933	$377,866
15	$42,621	$106,553	$213,103	$426,207
16	$47,819	$119,549	$239,096	$478,192
17	$53,400	$133,502	$267,002	$534,004
18	$59,383	$148,459	$296,917	$593,833
19	$65,788	$164,471	$328,940	$657,881
20	$72,636	$181,591	$363,179	$726,358
21	$79,949	$199,873	$399,743	$799,486
22	$87,750	$219,376	$438,748	$877,497
23	$96,064	$240,160	$480,318	$960,636
24	$104,916	$262,291	$524,579	$1,049,159
25	$114,333	$285,835	$571,667	$1,143,335
26	$124,345	$310,863	$621,723	$1,243,446
27	$134,979	$337,449	$674,895	$1,349,791
28	$146,268	$365,672	$731,340	$1,462,679
29	$158,244	$395,612	$791,220	$1,582,439
30	$170,941	$427,356	$854,707	$1,709,414

Goal Planning Worksheet

	Goal 1	Goal 2
What is your goal?		
How much time do you have until your goal?		
How much total money is required to meet your goal?		

Calculate Your Goal

	College Funding	Automobile Purchase	Retirement
Determine Average Cost			
How Many Years to Goal			
How Many Months to Goal (Years x 12)			
Amount Needed to Save if No Interest was Earned (Average Cost Divided by Months to Goal)			
Monthly Savings with Interest Earned. (Using 5% Money Chart)			

Sources

NCPA, Survey of U.S. Trust Corp, *Wealth Inheritance and estate tax,* no.289 Sept. 21, 2006

U.S. Department of labor – Bureau of statistics, *Occupational employment statistics*, May 2009

U.S. Dept of Commerce – Bureau of economic analysis, www.bea.com

Employee Benefit Research Institute, *The 2010 annual retirement confidence survey,* www.ebri.com

U.S. Department of education, *National Center for educational statistics, 2007-2008 school year data*

USA Today/Gallup Poll, April 20-23 2011, *Survey of children's future*

Rasmussen Reports, *National telephone survey on quality of life for children*, June 29-30, 2011

Internal Revenue Service, United States Department of the Treasury, *2010 Federal Tax Rate Schedule*

Internal Revenue Service, United States Department of the Treasury, *Publication 950 (12/2009), Introduction to Estate and Gift Taxes*

Bestsellers from ACS Books

The ACS Style Guide: A Manual for Authors and Editors (2nd Edition)
Edited by Janet S. Dodd
470 pp; clothbound ISBN 0–8412–3461–2; paperback ISBN 0–8412–3462–0

Writing the Laboratory Notebook
By Howard M. Kanare
145 pp; clothbound ISBN 0–8412–0906–5; paperback ISBN 0–8412–0933–2

Career Transitions for Chemists
By Dorothy P. Rodmann, Donald D. Bly, Frederick H. Owens, and Anne-Claire Anderson
240 pp; clothbound ISBN 0–8412–3052–8; paperback ISBN 0–8412–3038–2

Chemical Activities (student and teacher editions)
By Christie L. Borgford and Lee R. Summerlin
330 pp; spiralbound ISBN 0–8412–1417–4; teacher edition, ISBN 0–8412–1416–6

Chemical Demonstrations: A Sourcebook for Teachers, Volumes 1 and 2, Second Edition
Volume 1 by Lee R. Summerlin and James L. Ealy, Jr.
198 pp; spiralbound ISBN 0–8412–1481–6
Volume 2 by Lee R. Summerlin, Christie L. Borgford, and Julie B. Ealy
234 pp; spiralbound ISBN 0–8412–1535–9

The Internet: A Guide for Chemists
Edited by Steven M. Bachrach
360 pp; clothbound ISBN 0–8412–3223–7; paperback ISBN 0–8412–3224–5

Laboratory Waste Management: A Guidebook
ACS Task Force on Laboratory Waste Management
250 pp; clothbound ISBN 0–8412–2735–7; paperback ISBN 0–8412–2849–3

Reagent Chemicals, Eighth Edition
700 pp; clothbound ISBN 0–8412–2502–8

Good Laboratory Practice Standards: Applications for Field and Laboratory Studies
Edited by Willa Y. Garner, Maureen S. Barge, and James P. Ussary
571 pp; clothbound ISBN 0–8412–2192–8

For further information contact:
Order Department
Oxford University Press
2001 Evans Road
Cary, NC 27513
Phone: 1-800-445-9714 or 919-677-0977
Fax: 919-677-1303

Highlights from ACS Books

Desk Reference of Functional Polymers: Syntheses and Applications
Reza Arshady, Editor
832 pages, clothbound, ISBN 0–8412–3469–8

Chemical Engineering for Chemists
Richard G. Griskey
352 pages, clothbound, ISBN 0–8412–2215–0

Controlled Drug Delivery: Challenges and Strategies
Kinam Park, Editor
720 pages, clothbound, ISBN 0–8412–3470–1

Chemistry Today and Tomorrow: The Central, Useful, and Creative Science
Ronald Breslow
144 pages, paperbound, ISBN 0–8412–3460–4

Eilhard Mitscherlich: Prince of Prussian Chemistry
Hans-Werner Schutt
Co-published with the Chemical Heritage Foundation
256 pages, clothbound, ISBN 0–8412–3345–4

Chiral Separations: Applications and Technology
Satinder Ahuja, Editor
368 pages, clothbound, ISBN 0–8412–3407–8

Molecular Diversity and Combinatorial Chemistry: Libraries and Drug Discovery
Irwin M. Chaiken and Kim D. Janda, Editors
336 pages, clothbound, ISBN 0–8412–3450–7

A Lifetime of Synergy with Theory and Experiment
Andrew Streitwieser, Jr.
320 pages, clothbound, ISBN 0–8412–1836–6

Chemical Research Faculties, An International Directory
1,300 pages, clothbound, ISBN 0–8412–3301–2

For further information contact:
Order Department
Oxford University Press
2001 Evans Road
Cary, NC 27513
Phone: 1-800-445-9714 or 919-677-0977
Fax: 919-677-1303